From the Author of Amazon
"Top Biller – The Life

Dear Gabi

Thank you !

All the best

Steve 27/09/23 .

THE
GUEST
LIST

Steve Guest

Printed in the United Kingdom
First Printing, 2023

ISBN: 978-1-9162459-4-5 (Paperback)
ISBN: 978-1-9162459-5-2 (eBook)

SGuest Publishing
Walsall, WS9 0DN

steve@sguest.co.uk

Contents

ACKNOWLEDGEMENTS   5

BRITISH HEART FOUNDATION   7

FOREWORD   11

ABOUT THE AUTHOR   15

INTRODUCTION   17

CHAPTER ONE: ADAM LAWRENCE   25

CHAPTER TWO: CHRIS O'CONNELL   41

CHAPTER THREE: GREG SAVAGE   55

CHAPTER FOUR: JAMIE YORK   79

CHAPTER FIVE: JEREMY LAZARUS   99

CHAPTER SIX: JO BRITTON   115

CHAPTER SEVEN: LEE ELDRIDGE   137

CHAPTER EIGHT: MICHAELA WAIN   155

CHAPTER NINE: MIKE AMES   171

CHAPTER TEN: SIMON THORPE   189

CHAPTER ELEVEN: MIKE WHATMAN   205

CHAPTER TWELVE: JEREMY SNELL   221

CONCLUSION   235

Acknowledgements

'The Guestlist' is my third published book. Wow!

This milestone marks a crazy moment in time as I go through the journey of life, putting myself 'out there' and navigating the ups and downs as a business owner, author, podcaster, YouTuber, husband, and father. It's a fantastic journey that I embrace wholeheartedly, BUT I couldn't have achieved even half of it without the people that motivate, inspire, challenge, direct, and empower me.

Those people are the backbone of this book.

Surround yourself with the right people, and
the journey becomes much better.

As always, I wish to thank my wife, Emma, who supports and backs everything I do, including all the successes *and* the failures. A huge thanks to my two boys, Ethan and Hugo, who motivate me to keep motoring on. I must thank Emma, Tom, and Kris at work for bringing the banter and accountability to stay ambitious, think big, and grow.

A colossal thank you is due to Peter Morgan from MonkeyPants Productions, who painstakingly edited each podcast episode and helped with the launch, the framework, and the final production of each episode. Pete also narrated and produced the audio versions of my two previous books, 'Top Biller – The Life of a Recruiter' and 'A Personal Brand Story', for which I will forever be grateful. It's tough to explain the difficulty of recording the audio for an unabridged version of a book unless you've attempted it; it's an artwork.

Of course, a huge thank you to the amazing people featured in this book. I would have never been able to create 'The Guestlist' without the guests who contributed their valuable wisdom. Recording 'The Guestlist Podcast with Steve Guest' is great fun; it allows me to take time out from the recruitment day job and spend time with hugely successful people. During the 1-2-1 sessions, while recording each episode, every guest told me about their journey, talked about the lessons they learned, and gave me advice, support, and ways to learn more. Then I get to share all that with our listeners and viewers—what a bonus! Thank you so much to every one of you.

I cannot stress this enough; in all that I have ever done and achieved, I've learnt to keep the good ones close and try to share some of the knowledge along the way.

As always, a huge thank you goes out to my editor-in-chief, Claire Robbin, who always ensures my words make sense and flow with a level of eloquence that I could only dream of. Another big thank you to my self-publishing expert, Sam Pearce of Swatt Books. I am also hugely grateful to my proof-readers Rhys and Kyrie.

I am truly thankful for everyone who has made this book possible and humbled that so many successful people have shared a piece of their story so I can share those stories with you.

I am 100% confident you will find value in the content, and I look forward to hearing your stories of success.

British Heart Foundation

It was easy to decide which charity I wished to donate ALL the profits of The Guestlist book to. It was always going to be the British Heart Foundation.

Back in 2002, I hadn't long returned home from working abroad in Fuerteventura. I moved back to the UK to live with my father and his partner for a few years (or at least until I had figured out my life and career), as I had spent two years working abroad and three years prior living and studying in Oxford for my degree.

In 2004, the May bank holiday weekend, my dad said he had woken up with pains in his left arm and shoulder, so much so, he couldn't put 'the bins' out on a Sunday evening. He asked if I wouldn't mind doing it for him. I said, "Of course, no problem". He then went to bed, only to wake up the following morning asking to be taken to hospital as he didn't feel too well. I remember so many parts of the day, the times he asked to go back home as his struggles were 'probably nothing'.

I convinced him to stay, and we moved from one hospital to another as they didn't have the right equipment; we finally got checked in, and he was given a bed. After several tests, they advised that my dad had probably had a couple of mild heart attacks, at some point over the previous 12 months or so, that had gone by unnoticed.

My dad had started coughing up blood, which is obviously not a good sign; the doctors believed he had a leaky valve in his heart and needed further investigation. It was advised that they needed to do a routine 'transoesophageal echocardiogram' where they would put a camera down my dad's throat to photograph and examine his heart. It all happened so quickly. One moment he was simply going into the procedure, so we gave him a kiss, told him we would see him soon, that it was all routine and there was nothing to worry about.

And then at the point of the camera being put down his throat, my dad suffered a massive heart attack and sadly passed away.

I will never forget the silence and devastation that filled the waiting room as the doctor returned to tell us that our dad had sadly passed away. It crushed us.

This was a very poignant moment in my life that has continued to remind me to enjoy every minute—to make things count, take risks, live life to the full, and try to maximise my potential every day. No ifs or buts; to just go for it.

We have always had a history of heart-related issues; my brother was born with a hole in his heart; I take three lots of medication daily for blood pressure and cholesterol; and my father-in-law suffered a heart attack some years ago and has now fully recovered with a number of stents fitted. A school friend and one of my close friends' groups suffered a heart attack last year at just 44.

These instances have shown me that I needed and wanted to give back somehow – The Guestlist book creates an opportunity for me to do just this. Give back.

Thanks to British Heart Foundation for all that you do.

Rest in peace Dad x

Foreword

by Pete Morgan

The first time I met Steve face-to-face was at a local cafe back in 2020. In fact, looking back at my diary, it was Valentine's Day!

I'm still a little upset that neither of us thought to bring flowers.

From that first meeting, though, one thing was clear: Steve's drive and determination to succeed at whatever he turned his hand to were immense and contagious.

That meeting was to talk about the audiobook for his first massively popular and best-selling book, 'Top Biller', but our conversation also covered his desire to create a podcast, and that's how our working relationship with The Guestlist podcast was born.

Over 91 episodes, Steve educated, entertained, inspired, and provoked more thoughts than I've had hot dinners!

His approach to the podcast was refreshing; he understood the medium to a large degree, so Steve knew that if he were going to do it, he would have to commit to it, and my goodness, didn't he just? Not many business podcasts could consistently create valuable content week in, week out for two years solid. So, working with Steve on The Guestlist was a real treat.

We had a few conversations about what the podcast should sound like, who it should be aimed at, and what the content of each episode should be. These are conversations that I've had with almost all of my clients, but Steve had a fresh, different approach.

Instead of creating something that could have just been a nice ego trip, Steve was adamant about making episodes with something important to say and giving value to the listener.

I have a confession to make at this point. I honestly thought that Steve would be doing a straight-up recruitment podcast, which would interest people in the industry but hold nothing for the general public.

You can't see this, but I'm shaking my head and feeling a little ashamed.

[margin note: — Not just rec. industry. — Inspire Business]

Steve brought innovation to the business podcast. The guests weren't his friends or people from his immediate network; they were global influencers, industry experts, and business specialists. They were thinkers and doers, guests who, like Steve, had something to share with the audience – and couldn't wait to pass on their knowledge.

The other innovation that Steve brought to the business podcast was variety. The Guestlist, despite the name, was more than just guest after guest after guest.

As a seasoned podcast producer, I can tell you that this format *can* become a little like white noise.

Instead, Steve would spend an episode with a great guest and then shake it up by having a solo episode the following week.

[margin note: Solo + duet]

The solo episodes were just Steve, talking through his approach, mindset, and takeaways; from work, life, and everything. But, again, this wasn't vanity; instead, he wanted to share something of value with the listener, passing on knowledge for the betterment of others.

As I said, Steve knew the medium of podcasting. He knew that the value in producing a business podcast lies not in "Look at me, look at me," but in saying, "Look at this great guest – who is speaking to me. I clearly have influence and know what I'm talking about." Having a podcast isn't about the ego; it's about confirming that you are an expert in your field – and creating a bond with your listener that is stronger and more intimate than so many social media posts.

Think about it – podcasting is a solo pursuit. You don't sit around in a group listening to a podcast. You do it while you're on your own – commuting, walking the dog, at the gym, and getting into bed at night. It's just you and the podcast. That's why I call it 'intimate'.

Looking back at those episodes now, The Guestlist was one of those rare times as a podcast creator and producer that I gained value from what I was editing.

When working on a podcast episode, I'm listening from an editing point of view and keeping an ear out for stumbles, gaps, and umms and errs; I'm not explicitly listening to the content. That changed pretty quickly with The Guestlist. I would listen through it first, as an editor and producer, and then I would listen again – to attain the knowledge – that nugget of value – that compels listeners to return again and again to good podcasts.

The amount of education and value coming out of each episode, featuring people I wouldn't have considered listening to initially, was game-changing. And the value just kept coming.

I now have a proper schedule for my working day, week and month – that guidance came from Michaela Wain. I changed my understanding of money within my business – that insight came from Jeremy Lazarus. I was introduced to and started using Social Selling – that was all down to Daniel Disney. I widened the subjects I read about; I bought more business books – and that wisdom came from Steve Guest himself in one of his solo episodes.

Only when you look (or listen!) to the 91 episodes as a whole do you realise the power of The Guestlist podcast; it's created a team of people that you can call on. By listening, you have surrounded yourself with the best people who can help you become a better version of yourself, and you'll realise it's true when you finish this book and go back and listen to the podcast.

Steve and every guest wanted to improve *your* business *and your* life. Everybody involved in the podcast and the book is thrilled by the value other people can now take away from it.

I'm so excited for you to get into this book! Think of The Guestlist as a mentor and cheerleader who will push you onward and give you focus. It is a rarity in business podcasts, where the value applies to your personal life as much as your working life.

So, enjoy the journey Steve and his guests have been on and the one these chapters will inevitably take you on. Hopefully, it will involve you making your *own* podcast!

Stop procrastinating – start podcasting.

Pete Morgan
April 2023

About the Author

Steve Guest is a seasoned recruiter with 18 years of experience recruiting commercial construction top talent across the Midlands. With a passion for empowering recruiters around the world, Steve founded the successful online recruitment training platform, '12 Week Recruitment Mastery Programme'.

As a best-selling author across multiple categories on Amazon, Steve has made a significant impact with his books, 'Top Biller – The Life of a Recruiter' and 'A Personal Brand Story – Top Biller to Global Mentor'. 'Top Biller' has become the highest-reviewed recruitment book on Amazon globally.

Steve's drive to add value and share his journey led him to host a podcast, 'The Guestlist with Steve Guest', where he invites industry experts to share their insights and knowledge.

Beyond his professional accomplishments, Steve's family remains the cornerstone of his life. He takes pride in knowing his WHY and what drives him forward daily. He lives by the mantra of building for opportunity, always studying, and looking to improve a little every day, even if it's those seemingly small 1% incremental moves forward.

Steve continues to inspire and empower others to achieve their full potential.

Why this podcast?
Who for?

Introduction

What is the Guestlist with Steve Guest Podcast about?

In true podcast style, The Guestlist with Steve Guest's 'about' goes a little something like this.

> "Welcome to The Guestlist with Steve Guest. Let's prove the doubters wrong and let's do it together – if you are someone that wants to show what you are made of, despite the rejection, despite the ridicule or your own fear holding you back then, you are in good company. Alternatively, if YOU are happy being comfortable, constantly sat in safe mode plodding along then this isn't the place for you.
>
> If you want to 'set the trend', free the shackles, rise above the rest and outperform the competition – if you want to set a trail of success and high performance and smash through your goals then stick around as this will an incredible journey. If you are here, then you are clearly seeking more from your journey through life.

You already know you have greater potential and a much bigger calling and that you need to spend more of your time around the right people. You know the type—the individuals that motivate, inspire, empower, and challenge.

That is why this podcast was created.

Come and join us."

And I couldn't have put it better myself!

Welcome to the world of The Guestlist, where we champion knowledge sharing and value adding. This book is for anyone who wants to expand their expertise, challenge their assumptions, and gain fresh insights that can transform their careers and lives. In the following chapters, we'll cover various topics with our guests – leaders in Recruitment, Property, Money, NLP, High Performance, Entrepreneurship, Management and Leadership. Although these subjects may appear disparate on the surface, I purposefully haven't put them into 'topic order' as they all share one crucial feature: the potential to offer valuable insights that you can apply across multiple industries and professions. By stepping outside your comfort zone and exploring new perspectives, you can unlock a world of possibilities to help you gain a competitive edge, drive innovation, and ultimately achieve massive success in your field. Whether you're a seasoned professional or just starting out, the lessons in this book will challenge you to broaden your horizons.

Why did I write this book?

I wrote this book after discovering, through my own personal branding journey, that people prefer to consume their content in different formats depending on the time of day and whether they are commuting, working out, or sitting on the beach. I recognised that The Guestlist Podcast provided a lot of value, and could reach an even larger audience in print. This book is a collection of wisdom by extraordinary people, all of whom provide incredible value and have greatly aided me along the way. If this book inspires anyone to think, "I want to create a similar journey," they can use it as a resource. This book is a guide of expert information and insight that will inspire anyone involved in business, recruitment, sales, property, and more.

When I was 35 years old, I decided to embark on a ten-year 'financial freedom plan.' It entailed many aspects, as I wanted to advance economically. So, I set aside a sufficient amount of time to surround myself with the right people, invest in various areas, and further my education. A large part of that process was to establish a recruitment business, improve my recruitment skills, invest in real estate, and work on my growth mindset and thought processes to ensure everything was in alignment. A significant portion of the advice in this book has positively impacted that journey, and I owe a debt of gratitude to many people along the way.

My ten-year plan, more of a life journey, was to educate myself and accumulate wealth in order to achieve goals for my family and provide better opportunities for our future. Many of the people I interviewed for this podcast actively supported and assisted me.

My ten-year plan was written and put together in February 2014, inspired by the birth of my son, Ethan, in 2012. It took me a year or two to wrap my head around what being 'a Dad' entailed before deciding to put together a plan that would provide Ethan with an abundance of opportunities. I never wanted to have to say, "We can't afford that," "We'll never be able to do that," or "That's never going to happen."

I'd rather face the possibility of 'failure' to protect Ethan as he grows up and show him the right way (if I found it) and the path to avoid if it was littered with disaster.

Ethan changed my mindset because I wanted to make more money, become more successful, and generate multiple income streams from various sources so that we could earn money even while we slept. I hoped that if we ever got into trouble, whether in business, health, or anything else, we'd be able to continue fulfilling and living a healthy and happy life having generated wealth from success – whatever that looked like. I called it the ten year 'Financial Freedom Plan', because to me, freedom meant having enough money to pay all of our bills and necessities, such as food and shelter, and make enough money to avoid exchanging our time for it. By the age of 45, I wanted to be in a position that whatever I'd invested in and created was generating revenue that met all of our needs, allowing us to choose where and how we spent our time. If that meant going away for more than two weeks and possibly spending the entire summer somewhere, I was all for it. Being a father and having more responsibilities makes you more dynamic because you're doing things for someone other than yourself. It evolved into a more determined motivation.

I began to educate myself. I began looking into Commodity and FX Trading, completed a 12-month mentorship programme, began investing in real estate, became a landlord, and learnt the art of buying low and selling high. I also began to read a lot more. I began by reading the autobiographies of successful people such as Sir Richard Branson and Lord Alan Sugar. Then I started reading motivational books by well-known entrepreneurs such as Tony Robbins, Darren Hardy, and Gary Vaynerchuk. I discovered that the more I surrounded myself with people who had found success and wealth and created assets that generated multiple revenue streams (both personally and virtually), the more their philosophies became a part of my journey and gave me a growth mindset.

One of the goals of 'The Guestlist with Steve Guest Podcast' was to find people who are wealthy, successful, and masters/experts in their fields. I wanted to talk to them to learn how they achieved their success.

Everything has the potential to be 'an opportunity', but you must be willing to take educated risks and move forward. One of my personality traits is that I am extremely risk averse – I never want to jump in with both feet and usually want 'all the information' before taking action, which isn't always possible or plausible. So knowing that you have the right people around you to ask the right questions and get the best answers made it much easier to make informed and better decisions.

I am releasing this book nine years into my plan, raising the question, "Will I meet my ten-year financial freedom plan?" Of course, you could argue that I'm not far off. It remains to be seen whether I will hit my target, but one thing I know is that I am in a far better place now than I was eight years ago. It's just getting the journey going and having a plan to start – this is the most important stage!

I've taken action in every area, and I've increased our wealth and achieved success in everything I've set out to do. This includes starting a recruitment business, investing in real estate, and investing in stocks and shares. My recruitment firm now employs five people. I've written two books, one of which has become a worldwide best-seller. Every Friday, I release a podcast episode that is currently downloaded across 40+ countries. I'm in a much better place than when I started eight years ago. My actions have enabled us to do things that I would never have been able to do if I hadn't started the journey and put pen to paper.

However, accomplishments aside, I've realised that the journey has been the most important aspect. The ten-year plan is excellent to have in place, and I've been completely motivated to achieve the end goal, but as the end draws nearer, I realise that goals change, and the desire to achieve certain things changes as you get older. We only had one child when I first devised the ten-year plan, but now we have two – Hugo and Ethan – which adds new dimensions. In retrospect, it was and still is ALL about the journey.

Will I be happy if I achieve my ten-year plan? Of course! But, I won't be disappointed if I don't. When I look back over the last eight years, I'm extremely proud of where I am now. So, I'm not concerned whether it comes to fruition or not because I've learnt so much along the way. It hasn't been all about success; I've learnt a lot from the parts that didn't work, and that has been a huge part of the fun. The journey has taught me that you never have all the answers, that timing is never perfect, and that sometimes you just have to react and act. You can deal with the questions, problems, roadblocks, setbacks, and failures along the way, allowing you to make better decisions the next time.

I believe you require a plan, whether it is a month plan, a three-month plan, a six-month plan, a 12-month plan, a five-year plan, or a ten-year plan. When you put things in place (and write them down), you have something to strive for, which provides clarity and focus. However, don't be too hard on yourself if you don't quite meet your goals because the journey is far more important than the destination. While it's satisfying to say, "I did it," things will change. For example, when (and if) I reach 45 and haven't achieved every goal, I'm not going to sit down and feel sorry for myself, thinking, "That was a complete waste of time. What have I accomplished in the last ten years? ". Instead, I'll examine everything and think, "What am I doing? What have I accomplished? Where am I going? What have I failed to achieve? How long will it take me to accomplish what I haven't already?" and then devise another strategy and plan. The important thing is to keep going.

How should you read this book?

The advice in this book is not industry-specific; it is not simply a book on recruitment, property, or wealth; instead, it is a book filled with incredible wisdom from people I've met—people who have provided inspiration and motivation on my path. I feel strongly that the contents will add incredible value to your life and business.

However, one of the most common themes across all chapters is mindset. At some point, all the guests had a breakthrough and realised that a mindset adjustment had improved their lives and businesses. 100% of the people I interviewed for this book have never given up on their dreams, and neither should you. Take what you can from the wisdom in these pages, and most of all, enjoy!

Steve Guest

CHAPTER ONE

Adam Lawrence

(Property)

About Adam

Adam Lawrence has been involved in over 500 property deals in the past decade and built a substantial residential and commercial property portfolio. Adam has joint venture experience that runs into eight figures worth of deals. He has bought and sold limited companies with property assets in trading businesses, co-owns multiple investment companies, asset management companies and letting agencies as part of the business portfolio. Adam was Warwick Business School's top MBA Dean's List prize winner in 2012/13 and has delivered exceptional returns in a low-yield world with high-risk management at the heart of all his ventures. His first degree was in Philosophy, Politics and Economics at Oxford. He has a diverse business background with a broad range of experience, specialising in devising strategies that can thrive in any economic environment. Adam has significant team leadership experience across business and non-profit consultancy projects and particularly enjoys solving business challenges.

In Adam's own words:

Steve: *I'm trying to think back, but I believe we started talking via LinkedIn around four years ago.*

Adam: Oh, I think it's more than that, Steve. I remember the building where you first came to have a coffee with me. And we left that building in 2016.

Steve: *I've obviously been enjoying myself too much! I reached out to you as I was looking at getting into property. I had sent out a couple of messages to potential mentors before I'd messaged you; I got a response back from a particular person who was willing to spend some time with me – someone who will remain anonymous as they wanted to charge me £500 an hour, plus the coffee. At that point, I thought it was too expensive – I certainly didn't have £500 to spend on property education, especially when I had zero understanding. So, I sent you a message on LinkedIn and said, "Could you spare me a little bit of time for me to come over and have a chat with you?" Which you duly did. We spent a good hour, maybe two, sitting and having a coffee. You told me the ins and outs, and you put an offer on the table. Can you remember what the offer was?*

Adam: Please enlighten me; I've been to sleep since then!

Steve: *Your offer was, "Okay, here's the deal. I need to go and see my properties. They are dotted in and around some of the East Midlands and some just north of the Midlands." I think the furthest we went north was Doncaster. You said that you would take me around your properties, spend the day with me, that I could quiz you all I like and that you would show me the wins, the losses, the problems, and the mistakes. You talked me through each of the properties and what had happened and where in a 24-hour period. It was a day's worth of education, for the cost of a pub lunch and a bit of petrol – easily one of the best investments I've ever made! What a bargain. Genuinely from* *the heart, I will be eternally grateful. In my experience, it's rare to have people willing to go to such lengths and spend time with someone they don't know. You didn't know me, other than from a coffee and a quick chat, but you started me on a property path that gave me the basics and confidence to get started.*

Adam: I really appreciate you saying that Steve, and I think it's important. You should always pay it forward. I was paying it back from other people I'd met since I started on the property networking circuit in about 2011, and I met a handful of good people who gave me a lot of their time and expertise. So, I thought, 'You know, it's the way forward, reach down and help people up'. And that's one of the reasons why we did what we did in the property networking sphere ourselves when we founded Partners in Property.

I was invited to this private networking meeting in Birmingham and thought, well, I'll come along and see what it's like. And there were some great people in the room, but it ran its course organically over 12 to 18 months, and then new people weren't coming in. Our main challenge is to balance bringing in a sufficient number of new people while maintaining a base of existing members to foster relationship-building. Like a breath of fresh air, new faces are valuable as they bring a new perspective. However, it's important to avoid overwhelming people by pushing them too much, as some educators might do. We strive to find a good balance where we can introduce new opportunities without overwhelming our members.

Being new to property doesn't mean you're new to business.

We get people who are new to property and perhaps just sold a business in their 60s, but they're coming to us to learn about property. Then some people have developed or acquired hundreds of units, sold them, or held them – a real spread makes for a rich discussion. We've had someone join recently who's experienced in his field – oil and gas – and he solves problems in a slightly different way. It's sting to hear his questions, from short leases to tenancy issues t better to have HMOs (house in multiple occupation) or serviced nmodation?' etc. I have learnt a lot by watching how people think, and I enjoy it as well. It challenges me. That's ultimately what I go there and spend my time doing. I want to be challenged, I want to continue improving myself, and I want to keep working through new ideas. And, of course, with the changing environment we've all had over the last couple of years, it's been healthy. Challenges are one of the things that's helped me work through the choppy seas.

Steve: *We need the challenges to offer up constructive debate. We don't always want people to always pander to us and say, 'Well, you're doing so well, or you're successful'. You want people that say, 'Well, why aren't you doing it like this? Or have you thought about doing it this way? Why are you going that direction?' So, Adam, your growth since we first met has been significant. Can you tell us more about that?*

Adam: When you and I first met, Steve, I had a block of 10 flats with two commercial units underneath, which was probably more than a quarter of the units that we had in the portfolio. It was a big purchase early on, which I bought with a business partner in 2014. I had a hairdresser underneath and a beauty salon as well. I was not even educated enough to understand the difference between the two properly, but they get on very well. They managed to survive COVID, which is great, and when you think about it, it's an interesting point. Ten years ago, some people would turn their noses up at salons and cafes, whereas now, in the 'experience economy,' it's actually the best stuff you can have on a high street. You can't get a haircut on Amazon!

Also, the male side of the grooming industry has shot through the roof in the last decade, so I like to think those shops have got longevity.

On Property

Steve: *I've dabbled in property. I couldn't sit here and say that I'm an avid property investor, but I've had a good few years where I bought a few properties which were bought in line with a potential exit in years to come. I've got a bit of a pension plan which is there for the kids when they grow up, so they've got a legacy to a certain degree. I've kind of fallen out of property the last couple of years with everything else that's going on, but I want to get back into it. What advice would you give to somebody who wants to get into property but they're nervous about buying a second property, or an investment property, that first buy-to-let or HMO? There's so much information out there, but some of it is good, and some is not. How do you take that first step? How do you manage the risk?*

Adam: A lot of people ask me about taking that initial plunge and the first step into investing in property, and I want to say it's mindset, but it isn't *100% mindset*. Your mindset needs to be in the right place – I've met many people who have educated themselves quite extensively, spent 10,000 hours and £10,000 to £100,000. But a lot of people, like me, prefer to learn by doing. If you start by looking at the mindset side, I've seen people spend all that money, not do anything with it, and not even take that first step. Sometimes people underestimate how big that first step is! It's a Neil Armstrong moment. I've done many hundreds of deals, but to be honest, the important thing for you is to start with one, and after one, there are two, and then there are three or four. And that's it ultimately. It doesn't have to be an arithmetic progression. A graph of Warren Buffett's net worth is a good example – it's really a pretty flat line, and then, when he was nearly 70 years old, it suddenly accelerates incredibly. I think it's a similar thing within anything that you do.

Educate Yourself

If you want to get started in property, there's a ton of great material on YouTube and a ton of bad material, but of course, it's subjective. I like listening to podcasts about the economy and hedge fund management because I'm genuinely interested. A lot of people would think, 'Blimey, I'd rather put a gun to my head than listen to all of that!'

Look at the agenda of the people providing you with the information and realise that some of the best free content isn't provided by the people who will protect your wealth in the best way, unfortunately. I think YouTube's the greatest educational resource this planet has ever seen. Similarly, if you read the papers, you have to read across the board. You've got to go from The Guardian to the Telegraph and a few bits in between, even if you don't identify with either of those polar opposites because you've got to read across the spectrum. I think with so many places to get your information from, YouTube makes the algorithms helpful because it points you in the direction of things of potential interest. Don't think that one person or one organisation is the holy grail because they're absolutely not. And you know, you've also got to translate it into what matters to you. Somebody based outside of the UK might not be interested in UK property – there are different legal structures and other things to consider. So, go in with an open mind. No big hamster wheel exists in the property world to make a million pounds overnight. There are small bites. There are HMOs, service accommodation, Forex, Crypto, and Amazon e-commerce. The reality is all of those things are legitimate ways to make money if you've got the right skill set, apply yourself in the right way and educate yourself. But you'll never master one of them if you try and do all of them at the same time.

Steve: *I went to an audience with Doug Ellis, and he said, as he regularly did, "An apple well bought is twice sold". As an ex-qualified Buyer, I'm very risk averse, and when buying that first property, I just got myself into a zone and thought that if I bought it well, then I would be halfway there. If the numbers work, then I'm almost there. As long*

as it's planned and prepped, and I've done what I think I need to do. If it
goes horribly wrong, it's a lesson, and you pay for the education on the
parts that you perhaps didn't do so well. But if you bought well, you're
reducing the risk and hopeful it will prove to be a solid investment.

Adam: Yeah, I like the analogy a lot. I think that property is full of clichés, as I'm sure most people will appreciate, but one that actually is often always true is 'don't wait to buy property. Instead, buy the property and wait.'

On Focus

I've already mentioned Warren Buffett once and love to go on about him. He talks a lot about focus rather than diversification for the sake of it. One of the questions we always ask people if they're going to get serious about property is, 'How many hours a week are you going to put into it?' I've talked with people who looked at getting into the property as something to do if they found the time and the money. You don't need both of those things necessarily at the same time. If you've got no money, perversely, the longer you go on, the less you need money. But if you've got time, you can still exchange some of that time for money, find people to partner with and the rest of it. But you need motivation. When you've got confluence in those three areas, I call that 'the danger zone'. I mean that in two possible ways. Number one, you could put yourself in danger because there'll be lots of people trying to sell lots of things to you that are high-ticket items. But it can also be quite dangerous because you've got time, money and motivation, and you can do a lot of damage in this space in a relatively short space of time. If you don't manage the risks correctly, you can lose money. People lose money in property transactions all the time, and it doesn't get spoken about, yet it needs to be spoken about. If you can learn from other people's mistakes, that's the ideal scenario. I've tried to do presentations about things that have gone wrong over the years, so people could see how it didn't finish me off. How I dealt with things when the chips were down, and to realise there's something to take away from that. You don't win them all. I mean, anyone who's done hundreds of transactions, who says they've won on every single one, is a *liar*.

Sometimes the skill is sitting on your hands and not buying and selling and buying and selling. You know, you can trade properties just like you can trade cars or apples, but it's a very high-ticket industry, and there's a lot of frictional costs with buying and selling properties, so that's where you want to get it right. Another cliche that I can somewhat identify is people who think, 'I've got £100k saved up. I'll be happy if I could make £1000 a month on that £100k. Now some of the problems I see is people putting that money into a House of Multiple Occupancy (HMO). And then when they've done that, they get their £1000 a month, but they don't think that they might have put £300k total, including the mortgage and everything else, into that project, and it's only worth £250,000. Note that income earned in your initial 50 months is taxable and reflects past work. This highlights the consequences of prioritising cash flow over wise purchasing decisions. You've got to think about what you want and why you want to do it. Do you want to protect wealth? Do you want to create wealth? Do you want to protect income? Do you want to create income? What are your drivers? If you don't know what your drivers are, then when the chips are down, you'll probably struggle with this as well.

I'd like to make a distinction between an investment business and a trading business here, as they are two completely different beasts. Most people want a trading business, and as I said, it could be cars, it could be apples, it could be houses, but it comes with overheads, and it comes with cycles. Whether they've got an estate agency or whether they've got a house renovation company, the stock doesn't come along in a straight line or in an orderly fashion. You know, it's the same as recruitment; it's the same as any industry; there are quiet times of the year and busy times. There are reasons for that seasonality, and it introduces a lot of debt. You have to come back to risk management, as it introduces a lot of variance. There'll be people who've bought the property and sold it over the course of the last couple of years, and the market will carry them forward so far. Look at London in the middle of the last decade as a good example. Everyone was a developer, and they were all making money, but the reality was that three-quarters of those people could have bought what they bought, locked the door, come back in nine months, sold it, made a massive profit and put no effort into it, because the market was carrying them. And then, in 2015 and 2016, most of them went broke or sold places cheap. Yet, the people who've been doing it for years, who are fairly sanguine and also good with their risk management, were okay. But everybody else didn't see it coming. Again, this comes down to education and spending time with the right people who have either been there, understand or know how to manage it better.

Network

During my MBA, I learnt from quality practitioners in their field, who had worked 25 years in corporate, and then moved on to teaching people because they had made their money and were happy. They liked the idea of being a professor in a business school, and they were absolutely fabulous. I learnt so much from that, but I also learnt that it was about a third of the value of that degree, realistically. The next third was the network around you. So, you had what they called exec MBAs, who were in executive positions; chief financial officers, chief execs, all sorts of people who would come and do a week, every eight weeks at the business school. It's several weeks in a job, one week at the business school, and you would do a module with them, and that was an incredible experience. Of course, the Business School is super well-connected from a networking perspective. And then the final third was soft skills, where a lot of emphasis is put on influencing, in terms of negotiation and self-awareness. People sometimes say to me, 'I spent £20,000 on a course, and I didn't get much out of it'.

And I say, 'Well, just before you beat yourself up too badly, just remember to make the most of the network surrounding you and make the most of furthering your soft skills. You can pick the educational part of the course over time, and you'll have all your resources. But don't give up because you haven't wasted your money. But you have got to work out how to utilise all of those tools at your disposal, and you've got to network.'

I think if you can identify people who've got similar values to yourself, that's key. You want to work with people with different skill sets, people in different situations, and people who will challenge each other because that's valuable. I think you need to have similar values because you will come up against tough commercial decisions, and things will only happen if you can align your values.

On the Journey

Steve: *What would you say has been a single turning point that has made you go in a different direction and served a large lesson?*

Adam: The biggest lesson or failure would be from underachievement, in many ways or another. I'd say the two key things that have happened to me are:

1. Getting in with the right group of people – that was absolutely key.
2. I had a fear of using fast finance or bridging finance.

I thought, 'It can't possibly be worthwhile. If the interest rates are too high, it's just too scary to do it.' And of course, since I started taking this seriously in 2011, a bridging loan in 2011, and a bridging loan in 2020, are two completely different things because of the interest rates and because of the competition in the market. So that unlocked the ability to stretch my equity. I'm primarily quite risk averse; I didn't want to take that second step and sought advice from six to seven people. It was really helpful getting their take on it.

Steve: *I love reading your posts because it engages a part of my brain that doesn't get used as often as it should. I love all of that because I know that you will stack the numbers and manage your purchases with a proper understanding of the elements and the risks. I think far too many people that get into property rush past the excitement of "Oh, we're going to have a property." And don't always necessarily look at all the risks and the 'what if' scenarios.*

Adam: Some years ago, I came in one day and thought, "I'm going to write a book; I'm going to follow in your footsteps. I'm going to write at least one book, and the first one's going to have to be about my Four Pillars of Investment. It'll be about your deal pipeline, where to find property deals from and what makes them good. And the second one is about finance and remaining financially attractive to lenders, whether they be high street banks, specialist lenders, or private lenders, because you can show that you make money." So, if you're not using debt, then you must be getting a lot of money from somewhere else and just ploughing it into property. And that's fine if you've got a fantastic business on the one side making millions of pounds a year; you can afford to do that. We've been in an environment now for 10-plus years where the base rate has been below 1%. And now we're in an environment where inflation is high, at above 3%. In a scenario where you don't need to borrow money, and there is a high inflation rate compared to the cost of borrowing, it means that, in real terms, you are essentially being paid to borrow money. In such a situation, it would be advantageous for you to take advantage of this opportunity.

Conversely, if you are saving money, especially in your older years when you might not have access to a building society or similar financial institution, you end up losing money each year due to inflation. This creates a transfer of wealth from the risk-averse older generation to business owners who strategically utilise debt to their advantage. And that's a key part – remain financially attractive, be financially savvy, and lenders are going to want to talk to you when you borrow millions of pounds from banks. They will want to interview you and know what you're talking about. So, reading the old Sunday supplement that I write up on the 'Partners in Property' Facebook page is a good way to stay savvy. It drives me to do the research and look into what I probably wouldn't do every week if I didn't write the supplement. I do have a genuine interest, but it keeps me accountable to do the work, especially now I know that many intelligent people are reading it. If I write a load of rubbish, I will be held accountable. It's a symbiotic thing, and that's why I enjoy doing it.

Steve: *All credit to you as well because I think, by nature, a lot of us don't educate ourselves or spend that time in the areas we should. There's so much out there and so many things that can distract us or take us down different paths, and the ability to understand where we can be highly effective and strategic is paramount and highly valuable. We often get lost in the momentum and the motion of doing our daily duties, whatever they might be, and don't spend the time to reflect and look back at where we are and where we're headed. So, to my next question, who are your influences in life?*

Influences

Adam: If I'm to go for the famous inspirational ones, then obviously Warren Buffett. I think what I admire about him, from a technical perspective, is that he's a very good manager of risk. Anything can happen in this world. People say you make your own luck, and I don't really agree with that, but I agree if you can avoid bad luck, then you make your own luck. Buffet's mantra is 'mindset in everything that he does.' He's taken very small risks and made huge gains. I also admire that he does what he loves. And he still does it at 90+ years old.

I work closely with Rod Turner these days, who has done a lot in property. He's great because he keeps me sharp. He keeps me accountable. I get energy from talking to him and working with him. We look at the world in quite different ways sometimes, and again, that's powerful because it gives us two sides of the same coin.

Ross Harper is someone I pick out from the property space as well because Ross has done so many deals and is so generous with his time. He's done some incredible things outside of property, also. He's brilliant with people and business ideas but terrible with detail. He is strategically amazing, and is the best problem solver I've ever met by a factor of 1000, but until six months ago, he didn't own a laptop. He's good at getting people in the right place to ensure businesses run smoothly. He has an eye for talent as good as any I've ever seen. He has 1000 ideas before breakfast, but he knows how to pick up the one or two that have actually got some legs and some mileage. He would tell you himself, 'Not everything I ever touch will turn to gold, it's how you deal in the negative times and the bad situations, and also how quickly you extricate yourself from something that's not going very well, you're not enjoying, or adding any value to your life.' I think that a lot of people could use that mindset – if you can avoid bad luck, you can go out and make your own luck and do what you want. It's not going to be easy. Because if it was easy, everybody would do it. That said, you can do it!

Steve: *What is one single piece of advice you would give?*

Adam: One piece of advice I have for people is to do what makes you happy. You're only here once. Some people are lucky as they are happy in a business, and some people are very unhappy because they get obsessed and can't do anything else other than work. Balance has to be there. The most important thing is balance. It's not just work-life balance – balance as much as you can in your life. If that's your goal, you'll be happy.

Adam Lawrence – In Summary

- Empower others by paying it forward – lend a hand and lift someone up with you.
- Being new to property doesn't mean being new to business – tap into your entrepreneurial mindset.
- Embrace challenges – they spark constructive debates and fuel growth.
- Keep your focus on growth and what motivates you to reach new heights.
- Getting into property is all about mindset and risk management – set your goals, research your market, and build a strong team.
- Partner with a reliable solicitor and accountant to navigate the complexities of property investment.
- According to Adam, success in business is one-third knowledge, one-third networking, and one-third soft skills development.
- Build a strong network of people with similar values and diverse skill sets to tackle challenging decisions together.
- Adam's biggest lessons: surround yourself with the right people, overcome your fears, and manage risks to take advantage of opportunities in property investment.

Contact Adam

https://www.linkedin.com/in/adamglawrence/
https://adamxlawrence.co.uk/adamlawrence
www.partners-property.com

Adam's Q&A

What's your version of success?

Very simply, the freedom to choose.

Top three books to read or listen to?

The E-myth – Michael E. Gerber
Superforecasting – Tetlock and Gardner
Thinking, Fast and Slow – Daniel Kahneman

What's your favourite quote?

"Focus on return OF investment before focusing on return ON investment".

What advice would you give your younger self?

Get out of your own way, and put yourself in as many challenging situations as possible, with as open a mind as possible.

What is the best investment you have made, and why?

Without a doubt in myself, in terms of personal development time – my MBA

What's your go-to productivity trick?

If it is under 5 minutes of work, do it NOW.

If you could write a book about your life, what would the title be and why?

"Building it from scratch" – because I started with no money, I only had my education.

What's one thing you're learning now, and why is it important?

Balancing focus on personal wellness, business, family and personal development. A difficult juggling act!

Who would you choose if you could trade places with anyone for a day?

Warren Buffett's brightest mentee!

CHAPTER TWO

Chris O'Connell

(Recruitment)

About Chris

Chris hosts the Purpose-Led Leadership Podcast, available on Spotify and iTunes. Chris is a global Top Biller and a £25 million recruitment business owner, and he is now a Non-Exec Director for a number of businesses. He believes almost all business problems are people problems because people without purpose have no centralised reason driving them to perform. Chris coaches' leaders on how to build purpose-led businesses that perform by working with the best process vision, execution and harmonising your life with your work. Chris works with leaders to develop and deliver hiring solutions, enhance business development programmes and account growth, talent management, retention, leadership development, organisational development, build robust value propositions, marketing strategies and getting businesses for sale. An outspoken advocate of mental health mindset and self-care and a proud dad to three incredible boys.

In Chris's own words

Chris: That's quite an introduction – I almost believed it myself!

Steve: *It's been a couple of years since we've been chatting, hasn't it? How are you doing?*

Chris: Yeah, it has, and thank you – I'm honoured to be invited to your podcast. I'm enjoying this year so far, and I'm really excited about the future at the moment.

Steve: *This year, for me, has just been crazy busy, and you come back more motivated to achieve all of your goals and targets. What does this year look like for you?*

Chris: I think it will start with self-care, looking after myself, so I can serve others. My energy portfolio is growing; I've got a good platform there. I think looking at different revenue streams, building our coaching business, doing a subscription model as well, and I love giving back to the sector as well. That includes my personal brand working and elevating that as much as possible, collaborating with many people, and keeping myself in check. But it's not just about business. For me, as you probably know, it's about personal growth as well as spending my time more wisely. It's important that I measure what I'm doing both inside and outside of work. I'm going to be a stickler for incremental gains and improving daily habits.

Steve: *Yes, I'm a firm believer in incremental gains; I talk a lot about the Compound Effect by Darren Hardy and the 1%. It's a great book and has been a game-changer for me. Back in the day, I used to buy that book for every person that joined the team because it's important to keep that concept in mind. It's not about massive changes on a grand scale. Instead, it's making that one extra sales call and coming in 10 minutes early to beat the competition. I believe those small steps add up over a period of time.*

Chris: Absolutely. For example, I live in a fourth-floor apartment with a lovely view, and instead of getting a lift over the last few months, I've taken the stairs. My leg muscles are amazing now, and things like that have given me more energy and confidence, which, in turn, gives me more positivity in business. It's amazing. There are many different things that are linked to the compound effect just by making small changes.

Steve: *Absolutely! My goals and plans are on a spreadsheet I do every year between Christmas and New Year. I structure it in terms of what I want to achieve across various areas of my life, whether family, fun, work, business, finance, etc. Then it's broken down into a smaller scale that's manageable. I think half the problem these days is we all have these big ideas and big plans which are governed by what you see on social media, as per ‹the perfect lifestyle'. We try to get there too fast and then stop because it's never achievable, and that is all because there isn't a plan or process in place to get to that stage.*

Chris: I agree. Psychologically, if you can visually see that you've moved a notch on the dial, even if it's a tiny little thing every day, you're more likely and remain motivated to carry on doing those things.

Steve: *So, Chris, as an individual, you've been through one hell of a journey. I know that from previous discussions. Can you give me a bit of an insight into the 'Chris O'Connell of old' and how you got to where you are now? What are some of the changes and things that have happened to you that had a real impact?*

Chris: I'll go back to age two and give you a whistle-stop tour to explain why I've had a roller-coaster career. I was born in a caravan, and that became home. When I was three, I was hanging out in the caravan window naked; my brother raided the fridge, and my mum, basically abandoned us there all night. My dad wasn't emotionally intelligent or capable of looking after us. I was fostered for four years between ages three and seven. Dad worked on the railways and never had any money, so I got bullied at school and was called a 'pikey' because I didn't have any of the right clothes. Dad remarried, and his wife abused me as well. So, the first two female figures in my life weren't exactly good role models. It affected me psychologically, just as it would have anyone who had an abusive stepmother and their own mother abandoned them. It affected my mental health. I didn't enjoy school and felt very different, almost inferior. I was vulnerable, very shy, and I felt like a bit of a misfit.

I joined a business called Computer Futures, which was a company with a group of companies called SThree, one of the world's biggest and best-renowned businesses. They are a £1.2bn business with 5000 people across 60 offices in 20 countries. I started as a resourcer, quickly became a consultant and got 30 contractors running. I was the first fastest person ever to become the worldwide top biller across every single brand in that group, billing £700,000 a year and placing project program managers. I became a team leader, and director, managing about 400 contractors. I fell into recruitment; it was almost like a calling. I became very good at it and left that business in 2003 to set up my own business. I got it to 100 people, £25m annual turnover and won 14 industry awards. Three 3* best company awards in a row. It was simply one of the best-recruiting businesses out there; then, we did a deal with private equity, which I'll talk about later. I still felt very heavy at the time, and the private equity transaction I did went wrong, and I didn't get the pay-out I deserved. That business was worth around 20 million, probably 30 -35 million in its day. It was going north, but that went wrong and hit me hard. So, as you might imagine, being a very exposed CEO, then losing all of that, and watching daytime TV every day really affected my mental health. Then I got divorced, lost access to my children, lost my house, became addicted to gambling, and had some suicide attempts. Talk about having lost my way – quite badly! Eventually, I found a two-bed flat, and that was a real turning point for me – time on my own and a period of reflection. I looked back and thought, "Wow, what an achievement!". It was the first time I had felt that way. Before that, I had imposter syndrome and a lack of self-worth.

Over the last two to three years, I've returned to LinkedIn. Andrew Silitoe invited me to his webinar as a guest speaker, and I talked about vulnerability and leadership. I used that as the framework and story to return to the sector. Over the last two years, I've now used my story to build a following, a brand and a business.

I've got some great clients and do a lot on mental health as well. So, I've reinvented myself, and I'm happier now with the purpose, the fulfilment, the direction and the substance I've got as a human being.

The comeback has been worth the suffering because suffering has meaning. I'm a living, breathing example of that. I appreciate life and see things differently than before, in terms of having the ability to walk into any environment, shop, and buy £35k watches or whatever it was. I was reckless, and I was wild. Back then, however, I felt I had to put on a certain persona to be this gregarious individual. Now, I see it as a gift. At the time, I felt it was the worst thing that could ever happen to me or to have to recover from, but actually, it happened for a reason. I don't know where I'd be now if it hadn't happened to me. I might well be an alcoholic, homeless, or in prison. If I knew then what I know now, it would have been different, but I wouldn't change anything. I feel I'm a much better leader now than I ever was. But I must have done something right because the figures don't lie. And the people that have worked for me in the past, or most of my ex-colleagues, who have gone on to build their own multi-million-pound businesses, will back up what I say. That Timothy James was an amazing business – talk about legacy and purpose. Where do you go from there? So, that's a great shame in itself. But I think the bigger achievement now is doing what I'm doing, being open and vulnerable and giving something back.

Steve: *Wow, that's quite a story – thanks for sharing! In the same regard to vulnerability and openness, I've been in recruitment for over 18 years, and I think the environment has changed, with COVID giving it a softer element. That said, you and I both know that recruitment is an unforgiving industry at the best of times and in many ways, it's archaic in how people are treated. There are some incredibly old-*

school methods and ways within recruitment businesses where it becomes hard to manage in terms of the activity, the KPIs, and the pressures. Quite often, it's seen as a weakness if you say, "I'm lacking motivation, and I don't feel like I can do this today." Let's face it; it's a tough environment, the market has changed the landscape, and recruitment has become more difficult. Some recruiters don't know where to go, what to do or how to overcome those hurdles. What would you say to people that are reading this and are struggling? What sort of things would you suggest?

Chris: It starts with awareness and accountability. I feel that when you start to be honest with yourself, then better things happen. I feel that even though the industry has become more difficult, it has, in turn, become more human. If you ask me what I look for in a good recruiter, I'd say, processes, belief, and hunger, but also emotional intelligence. Harness your anxiety and vulnerability and use it as your superpower. Instead of being a corporate and business leadership consultant, you can win more business and develop yourself by having a framework for your day-to-day recruitment. People buy from people. It's a common statement, but look at the explosion of the personal brand! A glance on LinkedIn now and every other post is a selfie. I wouldn't shy away from that. Lean on your emotions; they're here for a reason. When you start being more open about talking to your boss, managers, colleagues, clients etc., you start to win hearts and minds.

Three or four years ago, I didn't necessarily have a coach or mentor, and I didn't collaborate with my competitors. Now, I don't see people on my LinkedIn as competitors but more as collaborators. I think that's really good. It's about being true to yourself and ensuring that you aren't something you're not. Whether you're a CEO or a cleaner – we're all human beings at the end of the day. The real authentic people you know and recognise their weaknesses, and they hire people who can deliver the stuff that they're not very good at themselves. I think you can learn a lot from other people.

I've removed myself from some of my ex-colleagues and old friends, who deemed tearing other people down to make themselves shine brighter as a good thing. But in fact, it's the opposite. It's such a draconian way of going about your life, isn't it? I've gained 40,000 followers in the last year. People I thought were my competitors, instead of shying away from them or getting negative about them, I started reaching out to them, saying, "Hey, I love what you're doing. Let's have a chinwag."

There's enough abundance to go around; the problem is I think some people do feel that they have a monopoly on everything.

A lot of people in my circle say that all the top people give away a lot of their wisdom for free. But they're paying it forward because it's reposited to them differently. So that is how you should look at it.

Giving something away isn't losing something – you can only gain from that. I believe that concerning the universe, you get back what you give out.

On Personal Branding

Steve: *How are you building your personal brand? What are you sharing, and what are you talking about?*

Chris: I've got three pillars to my content; leadership because I'm a leader, I've been a leader, and I advise leaders; mental health and recruitment. They're my three areas of expertise, and I swap and change those around and in different formats. So sometimes, it might be a video, it might be a poll, or it might be text. I think showing up in terms of putting myself out there, talking about my journey, my story, and having the courage in my convictions to realise I've actually built a really big business, and I've sold that. Now I'm a Non-Exec Director to 15 businesses, and that's quite a high profile and high-level role. I think back and say, "Wow, that's really good".

I think it's about embracing who I am and being confident. When teaching new consultants, it has the confidence to say, "I'm advising you, and what I'm saying is right". Don't water your advice down.

The more successful calls you make, the more successful you become, the more podcasts you host, and the more confident, slick and efficient you get. I've pivoted along the way. You must have an understanding of what your fortes are. For me, leadership, recruitment and mental health are my forte, and it's important not to deviate from these. So, don't be talking about interior design or construction if you're not in that space.

Empowerment Towards Staff

Steve: *In terms of leadership, what advice would you offer to those looking for motivation to leap over those hurdles and achieve greater success? What are some of the traits that individuals should be working towards and possess to offer empowerment towards their staff? What should they be looking for as a leader?*

Chris: It's about vulnerability and leadership. I think no matter how big your business is, you must understand the power a one-to-one meeting has as opposed to this carte blanche kind of leadership style. You need to understand what leadership hat to wear, to whom and when. I've always been on the premise of managing the individual or team because everybody's different, right? Some people like presentations, for example, some like KPIs, some like a firm management style, and some like a cuddle or nurturing. The key thing is to understand emotional intelligence. I feel that as a leader, you need to understand your strengths and weaknesses, be open about that, get the right people around you, and communicate and talk. You don't have to put on a persona because you're a leader – you don't have to be a certain type of individual. It's a real art; I think where leaders go wrong is that they get a bit too stoic to behave a certain way, and I'm afraid I have to disagree with that. I would encourage my people to feel comfortable asking me questions and challenge me as well. And it's a real art because if you do it too much the wrong way, you can be deemed as a soft touch. So, I feel it's down to awareness and emotional intelligence mainly.

Honesty and Transparency

Steve: *My leadership journey has certainly seen many mistakes – sometimes you get it wrong, and thus you must be strategic and consider how you will deal with things. I'm always open to saying, "You know what, I've actually made a mistake there, and I've got that wrong." Would you agree with that philosophy?*

Chris: Yes, being able to admit you messed up enables the other person to admit that they did too, and that's what you want in a leadership situation. You don't want to hear all the good stuff; you want to hear where all the pain points are.

One Single Piece of Advice

Improve, not impress. A lot of times, and I've been guilty of this, we post content, do things, and make decisions based on trying to impress somebody else. Actually, we should make those judgments, decisions, and choices to impress ourselves and improve ourselves. That's the biggest thing I'm learning around – before I make a decision, I ask myself, "Is it going to improve me and the affected people, or am I just trying to impress myself or somebody else?"

act Chris

http://linkedin.com/in/itschrisoconnell
Website : www.basemindset.com
Insta : chrisoconnellcoach
TikTok : chrisoconnellcoach
Podcast : Purpose-Led Leadership (Spotify & Apple)
Email : chris@basemindset.com

Chris O'Connell in Summary

- Incremental gains and the compound effect are essential concepts to remember when trying to achieve goals.
- It's crucial to have a plan or process in place to achieve your goals and to break them down into smaller, more manageable steps.
- Even if they seem insignificant, celebrating small wins can help you remain motivated and committed to achieving your goals.
- Personal growth is just as important as business growth, and spending time wisely and measuring your progress in both areas is essential.
- Embrace vulnerability and emotional intelligence: To become a successful leader and recruiter, being open and honest about your strengths and weaknesses is important. Emotional intelligence allows you to understand and connect with people better, which helps build relationships.
- It's important to identify your areas of expertise and create content around them to build your personal brand. This involves being confident in your abilities and sharing your journey and story with others.

- Rather than viewing your peers as competitors, try collaborating with them. This can lead to positive outcomes for everyone involved; there's enough abundance to go around.
- To succeed in recruitment, having a framework for your day-to-day activities is helpful. This can help you stay organised and win more business.
- Being authentic to yourself as a leader is important. Don't feel you must put on a persona to fit a particular leadership style. Instead, understand your strengths and weaknesses and communicate openly with your team.
- Sharing your wisdom and giving back to others can lead to positive outcomes for yourself and others. Remember that giving something away isn't losing something – you can only gain from that.

Chris's Q&A

What's your version of success?

Not the size of my watch, how fast my car is, what type of house I live in, how big my business is, or my title – I've had all of those. Success is the quality of my relationship with myself, my loved ones and my community. The positive impact and legacy I am leaving on others and will continue to leave on others when I am gone.

Top three books to read or listen to?

The Compound Effect – Darren Hardy
Think and Grow Rich – Napoleon Hill
The Untethered Soul – Michael A Singer

What's your favourite quote?

Happiness is an Inside Job

What advice would you give your younger self?

Happiness is an Inside Job (book by Sylvia Boorstein).

What is the best investment you have made, and why?

In myself – because it is myself that is worth the most, not any material item.

What's your go-to productivity trick?

Execute 3-5 of the most important things each day – the rest is a bonus; if it's too time heavy for low benefit, delegate or outsource it. Don't time manage – TASK manage.

If you could write a book about your life, what would the title be and why?

Redemption – because I lost everything materialistically, and now I have everything in terms of fulfilment and purpose.

What's one thing you're learning now, and why is it important?

I must fall in love with myself every day and treat myself accordingly, so others can do the same.

Who would you choose if you could trade places with anyone for a day?

My sons!

CHAPTER THREE

Greg Savage

Recitment

Recruitment

About Greg

Greg has achieved several accolades over the years, accumulated a wealth of recruitment knowledge and experience, and been recognised for his contribution to the Australian recruitment industry. Greg was made an honorary life member of the Recruitment Consultant Services Association in 2004. In 2011, he was awarded a special commendation by the RCSA for his outstanding contribution to the recruitment industry.

He was named the most influential Australian businessperson on Twitter in 2016 and the most influential recruiter in Australia in the past 60 years in 2015. In 2018, Greg was inducted into the Recruiter International Hall of Fame as an early adopter of social media for recruiting.

In November 2018, Greg was named one of LinkedIn's top voices. Some of you will follow Greg's industry blog, The Savage Truth, which is also the name of his book, an Amazon Best Seller in its category that has sold over 10,000 copies. His second book, 'Recruit. Way' was published in June 2023

Greg is a Board Advisor for 12 Recruitment and HR tech companies in Australia, Singapore, and New Zealand.

In Greg's own words.:

Steve: *A couple of weeks ago, I put a post out on LinkedIn and asked my network, who they feel is very influential within the market; somebody that can add value, who they would like to listen to about high performance, top billing recruiters, motivational leaders, inspirational coaches and mentors within recruitment, and your name continually popped up. I'm unsurprised, as I have followed your content for several years now, and I am delighted to talk with you today.* One of the main reasons I wanted to speak with you today is high performance and what you feel separates average performers from high-performing billing consultants. What are the actual keys to success?

High Performance

Greg: I get asked that question a lot. People often ask, "Hey, can you tell me a key thing I must do to be a great recruiter?"

But it's a flawed question because it's like me asking you, "What's the one thing you have to do to be a great parent, or what's the one thing that makes a great footballer?"

There is no one thing. It's a bit complicated and a nuanced cocktail of different things. So, I answer it by saying that there are four main areas you have to understand to become a great recruiter, and you must look at yourself in four ways. I'll list them, and then I'll elaborate on them.

The **first** is intrinsic attributes. Like a footballer, you can d
you want to improve. But you will only go so far if you don ﹀
raw, innate ability. So, I'll come back to them.

The **second** is attitude and mindset. There are different attitudes and mindsets of supremely successful recruiters. I was a good recruiter, not great, mind you, but you probably would have hired me. I have worked with far better recruiters, thousands in fact, and I've been running recruitment businesses for 40 years. You get to know many people in that period, so I've studied this and tried to dissect the question you ask, and it's boiled down to intrinsic attributes, attitude and mindset.

Then **thirdly**, there needs to be a track record of continuous learning. So, once you have a great view of the intrinsic attributes, you can have the right attitude, but then you've got to learn specific skills, and then there is the final thing.

The **fourth** area is the process, and the way things are done. And that is more art and craft than it is science.

While all challenging experiences can build character, recruitment reveals true character. You truly see the way people behave in recruitment. Resilience is a critical intrinsic attribute; if people don't have that in a job like this, they won't succeed. Other inherent characteristics include stamina, positivity and work ethic.

> *I don't believe that the best-performing recruiters work the longest hours, but there is no doubt that if this job were easy, all the stupid and lazy people would be rich, yet they're not.*

It's hard work. A significant intrinsic value you need, believe it or not, is a word you don't often hear on a job spec for a recruiter, and that word is 'empathy'. Empathy is an intrinsic attribute of a successful long-term recruiter. Empathetic to the fact that they're dealing with human beings, both with the candidate and the client, allows them to become highly skilled in influencing, which I'll return to later. So those are some of the intrinsic attributes, which is component number **one** of this rich cocktail.

Number **two** is attitude and mindset. Great recruiters take a long-term view. There are plenty of shooting stars in our industry. The guy who cut my hair the other day was a recruiter – everyone's been a recruiter at some point, right? But if you plan to succeed, you must take a long-term view and take care of important things like customer service, treating people with integrity, and investing in building relationships. Many recruiters, even those showing promise, are out of the industry three years later, or they've moved on to something else.

A good recruiter can build credibility
and is conscious of that.

This includes simple but crucial actions like doing what you say you're going to do and getting back to people when you say you'll get back to them. What it's not is building a shortlist of two great candidates and dropping in a few below-par ones under the misguided belief that it will make your other two look better. The client will see through the façade and think you didn't understand the assignment, which will crush your credibility. The main element of attitude and mindset is a little term I call 'recruiter equity', which is vital.

Recruiter Equity

Great recruiters and high performers have recruiter equity. The word 'equity' means a share of ownership. Great recruiters work with their clients and candidates to give them a share of ownership in solving the problem. The problem is, "I want a job, or I have a job to fill."

They believe top-performing recruiters add value. They are not apologetic about what they do. They know that they know more than their clients about recruitment, not with arrogance but with confidence in their service. Plenty of people kowtow to their clients, which ends up with the finance director telling the recruiter how to run the recruitment process. This is nonsensical. No disrespect to the finance director because, of course, the finance director is good at finance. The recruiter goes into the meeting not with arrogance but with a mindset and an ethos of, "I am here to help. I have value."

Therefore, they get equity in the process. That means the client shares the problem with the recruiter. "I have a hiring need'. But they also share the solution. Signs of you having equity in the process is the client giving you the job exclusively; the client takes your advice, the client interviews the candidates you refer to the client, and the client accepts your advice on things like salaries and speed and how to frame the conversation. The client then gives a debrief on every candidate, which is rare. So, in that case, you've got equity.

> *So great recruiters build what I call recruiter equity. It stems from a primary platform of self-belief: "I can help this candidate, or I can help this client". It's not arrogance; it's a mindset.*

So, we've covered **intrinsic attributes, attitudes and mindset**, and then there are **learned skills.**

Learned skills.

The basis upon which everything is built is 'influencing skills'. Great recruiters have influencing skills. I don't know whether people realise this, but from 2010, when the financial crisis was over, up to 2019, we had a huge boom. Ten years of the biggest boom I've been through in 40 years. It led to many recruiters making money by screening, shortlisting, matching, setting up interviews, and occasionally, no matter the placement, there was no consulting. Instead, it was resume spamming at pace; that's what it was. And you could make money doing that.

Covid stopped everything for a while, but then in that post-Covid rush, it was back to speed over quality in many cases.

Great recruiters have influencing skills, which apply to everything. I use the word influence, but I prefer the word selling, but people think the word 'selling' is ugly. 'It's a hard sell.' But how I use the word is something to be proud of. It means listening, assessing, advising, consulting, and creating outcomes for the greater good.

When qualifying a job order, plenty of recruiters will take a job order, either very briefly over the phone or get an email with job details, and then start looking for candidates. This is a calamity. It is transactional. And it is fraught with the risk of bad outcomes for all parties. How can you start looking for candidates until you know the job's scope or if it could be filled by someone who matches that job description? A good recruiter will qualify that job description and consult with the client, talking through salary, qualifications, experience required, and priorities. It is always a different looking requisition once it's been qualified. More "fillable".

It's the same with securing exclusive job orders instead of competing in the bear pit of multi-listed contingent job order recruitment.

Influencing skills are as crucial on the candidate side of our work too. For example, understanding a candidate's real motivations. Most recruiters interview candidates for skills, qualifications and work history. That's the easy part; a machine can do that reasonably well. But what the machine can't do is understand the candidate's real motivation.

Because here's a secret. Some candidates lie.

Sometimes a big lie. Some might say, "I used to work for X, Y, Z company" when actually they were in jail. It's infrequent for that kind of lie, and mostly that will come out soon. It's not being transparent on the more minor things that are the key. Every recruiter asks this of a permanent candidate. "Why are you looking to change jobs," then the candidate says, "Career advancement", and the recruiter writes that down. But it's not always true. Often when you dig, the real reason the person wants to change jobs is to work closer to home. So, they can get home by five o'clock and coach the kids' football team, which is a brilliant reason. The point is, as a recruiter, I don't *care* about the reason. I just need to *know the reasons* and work with the candidate *to rank the reasons* so that I can make a match. I like to say a great recruiter knows how to architect the deal. That's the phrase I use.

> **And when I say 'architect', it's because that phrase means planning, building, and creating, and those elements make a great recruiter. So, the value is not in matching which machines can do, it's not in referring, and it's not in setting up interviews – it's in influencing.**

It's in creating excellent outcomes on which we should coach our recruiters. That's what I have spent a lifetime coaching a recruiter on. It's probably one key reason the management teams I have worked with have successfully built recruitment businesses.

> **Somebody told me the other day that they counted 41 recruitment companies owned by people who used to work for me.**

I can't take any direct credit. They did the work, and lots of them were better at running businesses than I was. I think it means they've learnt from all my mistakes and are implementing some of the lessons we learnt together.

Summed up, *great recruiters have learnt the skills to influence the outcomes of the moments of truth in recruitment.* The moments of truth in recruitment are those moments where there's an interaction between client and recruiter or candidate and recruiter, where the recruiter can influence the outcome for the greater good.

So, I'm talking to a candidate about a job. The candidate says, "I've never heard of that company. So, I don't think I'll go for the interview."

"Well," I say, "just a minute, let me tell you a bit more. I've placed three people there. They are happy."

The candidate begrudgingly decides to go, and he loves it. He gets the job, and I made that happen. That's the value. That's a moment of truth.

Debriefing the candidate after they've been at an interview is another one.

Recently, I sat next to an experienced consultant, and she took a call. She spoke to a candidate 'Bob' who was giving feedback on an interview she sent him on, and then she said, "Look, Bob, I'm sorry to do this. I'm so busy, just email me your feedback, please."

I asked her, "Why did you do that? That is your moment of truth. You want to hear the tone of his voice. You want to be asking how long he was there. Was money raised as a topic? Who did you see? You don't know who he saw. You sent him to get interviewed by John Smith. But he might have seen three other people. Did they offer it to him? Did he like the people? Would he accept it, and at what salary?"

This is pre-closing, which you should be doing with clients and candidates all the way through the process. This is not new, but many recruiters lack the skill, as so much of recruitment has retreated behind digital messaging. *Great* recruiters manage those moments of truth.

Believe it or not, I've only given you **three** ways to success so far: intrinsic attributes, attitude and mindset, and learned skills.

And the **fourth** is 'process'.

Process

I'll give you the secret formula to recruiting success and what great recruiters always do, even if they can't articulate it the way I am going to; great recruiters work close to the money.

People get offended when I say that. I know it's not all about money, but money is our scorecard. It's not the best scorecard, but in this business, we haven't billed, and you haven't created the outcome we want. Not *money*, but people getting *jobs.* That's our reason for existence. So that's the scorecard. We've got to get people working close to the money; great recruiters work on the most fillable jobs. I was in a training session the other day, and a recruiter told me he'd got 20 jobs in healthcare. He said, "Greg, how can I get more jobs?"

"Well, how many of those jobs do you fill in an average month?" I said.

To which he answered, "Three."

I said, "You don't need any more jobs. You need to work on how to prioritise those jobs. You need to work on the most fillable, and that's by taking the job order in detail and understanding the client's point of pain. We want clients in pain; we want clients to say, "I'm desperate; it's causing me stress."

So, work on fewer jobs where clients are committed to hiring and where the salaries are appropriate for the expectations.

And the other thing is working on candidates who are not only going to get offers – that's the easy part – you've got to work with candidates who are going to *accept* offers. That's what people don't understand. I mean, we don't get paid for getting people offers. Instead, we get paid for people accepting offers. So that means great recruiters work very close to the money, they work with the job orders that are fillable, they work with the placeable candidates, and candidates you will place will have two things; the ability, skills, competencies, and communication skills to get job offers, and also the motivation to accept a job at a reasonable salary.

Here's the magic formula. I've been a recruiter for a long time; I've worked with the best recruiters, many far better than me. But I've also managed recruiters for a long, long time. So, whenever I found a recruiter going off course, a high performer becoming average, or a whole office not hitting the numbers, you could see the reason for the problem in this formula.

Success x Quality x Target market

Success in recruitment. Great recruiters have high activity and do high numbers of the right activities. Here's the thing, if you don't do enough stuff in this business, you lose. We know that KPIs and micromanaging have a bad rap. But the problem with KPIs is the way they are implemented by management that doesn't have a clue. Measuring what you do to get incremental gains is the right thing to do.

It's no different to football; if I take one shot at a goal in a game, the only possible outcome is if everything goes my way; if the God of football smiles on me, is that I could score one goal, right? If I take ten shots at goal, my likelihood of scoring goes up, but activity is not enough. If those shots all hit the corner flag, I will not score any goals. So, the formula is activity times quality. High activity and high quality. Related to recruitment, we want you to make a high volume of the critical things: whether that's interviews, client visits, getting resumes in front of clients, or getting people interviewed by clients. We want more of those; quality candidates sitting opposite the right client, and I've got to have done quality matching and pre-briefing on both sides of all those things. So, it's activity and quality.

The third factor is the target market; I need to do a lot of activities, do them well, and do them with the right people. So even if I interview brilliantly, and I interview 12 people a week, if I'm interviewing the wrong people who don't have the skills that people will hire, I will not be successful. I might do ten client visits a week, visiting tiny companies that haven't hired anyone since 1999. Or I am not meeting the decision-makers. No success.

So, activity, quality, and target market.

Steve: *That is an answer – there's so much value and content in there. And I think, certainly in the UK, I'm not sure whether it's the same in Australia; my experience over the last 18 years is that good, competent people come into the industry, you interview them, and you think they're going to do well as a recruiter. But many people fail and don't quite make the mark. Why do you think that is?*

Greg: It's a good question. I spent a lot of time in the UK. I lived there for a few years. I recruited there and owned a business there for ten years. I go over quite often and do speaking tours. There are a few components to it. The first thing is (and I've been guilty of this) we in this industry, funnily enough, are not particularly good at recruiting. An example. I've been in recruitment for a long time, with thousands working for my companies or me. How many reference check requests have I had in the last decade where people have asked me, "What do you think of this guy who worked for you for ten years?" It's happened about three times in 10 years. In recruitment, we need to improve our own recruitment. We don't recruit against those core competencies and those intrinsic attributes I identified here, and we don't look for the skills. We get taken with superficial things like how the person looks, the school they went to, the fact they've been in banking, they play rugby, they speak our language, so we hire them. But do they have resilience? Do they have empathy? Do they have excellent listening skills? They have a high IQ, but are they coachable? First off, we hire the wrong people, which is why people fail. Second, they fail because they are not given the proper support. We are deficient in our industry. Somebody told me, "I'm not going to train that person because most of our people don't work out in the first three months, so I don't want to waste my time training them."

I mean, really? We've got to take the other view – we hired them, we believe they're going to succeed, and we've got to put *everything* into helping them achieve. They need training and coaching, which are different things. They need constant goal-setting and feedback. You can't just put them in front of a video for an hour and say, "There's our top performer; watch him doing interviews, listen in and soak it up." I mean, that's all good, but it's not the same as detailed training and assisting people. It's measurement, coaching, role play, and feedback; repeat until we see improvement. You don't measure someone's ability to be a recruiter by their billing in the first three months. Somebody asked me yesterday in a board meeting, "What number should people have hit in the first three months for me to say whether they should stay on."

You and I, Steve, could start at a recruitment company tomorrow, and after three months, you could have made two placements, and I could have made none. It does not make you a better recruiter; we know that you can fluke it right, and you can get a bit of luck going your way, a referral from a senior person, or a juicy job gifted to you. So, you've got to measure different things in the first three to six months: coachability, hitting the targets, doing the small things well, the activity targets that you set, and their attitude and their bearing.

So, the newbies need all of that, but sometimes – they lack fundamental resilience and grit. We use that word in recruitment, but it means something different to me. Resilience to most people implies toughness, and a kind of macho quality, to submerge your emotions and just keep on ploughing on. That's highly valued in many recruitment companies. "Do 100 calls and get rejected but do one more because you might hit gold. And love the rejection!". It is all nonsense. I'm all for emotion in recruiting. I'm all for people hitting their heads against the wall and crying. I wasn't much of a crier; I was more of a swearer, and if I needed to go walk around the block, that's fine. We want emotion; we want placement dances when people are successful. Passion is good! We want high fives. If you're invested in this thing, the rewards are so high, and the failures are so low that emotion is natural.

Here's the thing about resilience. It's wasted emotion that destroys recruitment careers. Wasted emotion means carrying forward negativity to the following conversation. We all know people who, two weeks later, are still talking about the offer that was turned down. True resilience is having two offers turned down, having somebody be rude to you, and then having another piece of bad news thrown at you. Still, in the following conversation with a client, candidate, or colleague, you arrive upbeat and focused on that person—that is resilience. Lacking that is often the cause of failure, and being unable to learn influencing skills is the other issue.

There are three kinds of paths you can go down as a recruiter. One, you can learn all these things I've explained today (although we've only scratched the surface), and you can become a high-performing recruiter, and if you do that, you will have fun and earn money. Those are the only two reasons to come to work.

The second path is you can fail, find out you're not good at it, then you can leave, and you can become good at something else; you might become a Nobel Prize winner in something else. So, it's not a crime to not be good at recruitment; just preferably find out early and then go and do something else.

The third path is the worst – long-term mediocrity is purgatory. If you are an average recruiter, I don't know how you could do it because your successes don't outweigh all your failures. The positives don't outweigh the negatives. Most recruiters are filling one job out of four, meaning they fail 75% of the time. How long would I last as a brain surgeon if I failed 75% of the time? How long would I last as an accountant if my tax returns for my clients were wrong 75% of the time? Putting aside the failure rate, it's the constant hit to your self-esteem. I am not saying everyone has to be a superstar. I'm not trying to encourage lots of people to resign. Instead, you focus on the positives and work at becoming great because many recruiters plateau and stall and end up being mediocre. We need incremental gains to our skill set, client relationships, brand and every other component of our work, then recruitment becomes fun and lucrative.

Steve: *That leads quite nicely to my next question. I've worked and mentored lots of recruiters, and I've coached very high-billing recruiters. There always comes a time when they're really successful, they are the person everyone looks up to, and things are going in the right direction, and then you start to plateau. What essential turnarounds get you from a position to grab that next level?*

Greg: There are two reasons for what you described, and it's widespread. One is it's the company's fault. Companies spend all their time and training on underperforming people, trying to get them up to the average, and very little time turning the good people into great ones. If you spend time making the good recruiter great, it will satisfy many more clients and candidates.

> not just for new or under performing. How can best do better?

Distraction

At some point, most recruiters wonder whether they should be managers. That leads to a very bad thing: the highest biller becomes the manager because that recruiter hasn't been put on a program to go from good to great, which is the company's fault. The highest biller *may* be a good leader, but it's not necessarily true. The second thing is the recruiter's fault, complacency and hubris – believing your own bullshit, "I'm great. I'm billing more than anyone in this place. I can't get any better." You see it in the behaviour of some high billers, they become prima donnas, and once you get that mindset, you're closed to learning. So, in answer to your question, recruiters who go from good to great have a mindset of continuous learning; they are coachable and will take advice. And they are open to measurement. I used to love dealing with high-billing prima donnas. I'd say, "It's been a great quarter, you've had a great year, and you billed more than everyone else. However, it appears you actually filled one job out of three, which is lower than the average in the company, which is a bit weird, isn't it? That's a bit disappointing; imagine you're in the lowest quartile. What can we do about that?"

How many jobs do you have an that you actually fill?

"I'm not filling only one out of three!" They declare.

"Yes, you are," I say, "so let's get a bit more positive. If you can get one out of three to two out of four, you'll bill an extra $100,000 grand here, you realise?"

"Well, what can I do about it, Greg?"

"Well, I'll teach you about exclusivity and prioritising your job with some goals."

→ Spot time wastes
→ qualify better

Now that the top performer still has his cred in the company, he's also got this goal that has enthused him, partially because he wants to prove me wrong but mostly because he wants to get better. Measurability helps you to improve, which constantly means goal setting, mentoring, and giving people nano degrees. A nano degree is a 90-100-day self-taught subject. I do it all the time, right? I did it for blockchain. I've read everything I could about blockchain; I went on webinars and phoned up IT professionals. Sure, it didn't make me a blockchain expert, but after 90 days, no one could fool me about blockchain, and I understood it. I am doing the same thing now with ChatGPT. I taught these great recruiters that they need a nano degree to help them to sell exclusivity and learn how to brand themselves on LinkedIn. LinkedIn isn't a sourcing platform; it's a branding platform; if you become good at branding, it'll solve your sourcing, don't worry about it.

Mostly leaders in recruitment companies fail their high performers because they leave them alone. What we should do is work with them to take them from good to great or great to exceptional through a plan. The irony is that the most significant outcome is 'longevity'; the recruiter stays in the job, stays in the company, earns more, feels more self-esteem, and feels their careers are on track. Leave them in the corner, and you'll find that billings plateau and sometimes go backwards.

Steve: *Why do you think that is? Why do we, as recruitment businesses do that? Why do we leave our top, highest billers, our best performers alone? I know; we don't want to interrupt the process and stop them from billing. But why do we think, "We should just leave them because they're good as they are, they're doing well, and I don't want to rock the boat."*

Greg: I think there are several reasons. Most recruitment company owners are not good business managers and leaders. Now that's not a criticism. However, many people who start recruitment companies are a bit entrepreneurial, typically good recruiters and decide to branch out independently. And most of them don't have the coaching, the leadership, the mentoring skills, and those people, they need to go and understand that they are no longer recruiters, they're an owner, a mentor, and a manager, and they've got to improve their leadership skills.

Another reason is that we bow down to the altar of high billings in this industry and allow people who bill a lot to get away with a lot of bullshit. For example, we all turn up on time, except for Jack, because he bills a lot. We in this company always fill in the stuff on our ATS, but not John because he bills a lot. So, they begin to learn that they are some separate species, and that's how you create a prima donna. The owner then thinks if they interfere with the high biller, they will upset them, so they leave them alone. That's so wrong; you want to get closer to your good people. You've got to tell them when they're out of line and that they should set a good example – hold up a mirror to them. Owners don't want to rock the boat, but they should push their high performers because they will become exponentially better recruiters, will fill a higher percentage of your jobs, they'll have better relationships with clients, will get more repeat business, more self-esteem, more bottles of wine from happy candidates, and much more likely to love their job, which is really what our job as leaders is to do. We want people to be successful and love their job. So, they go together – if you love your job, you will likely be successful. If you're successful, you're likely to love the job.

Steve: *Love it. Over the last few years, I've been on my own journey, and I'm surrounding myself with mentors, whether literarily or face-to-face coaches, ensuring that I've got influential people around me. Over time, who've been the most influential people who have inspired you or pushed you to new levels?*

Greg: I started in recruitment when I was 21; my first job was straight from university in January 1980. Hard to believe, but over 40 years ago. I became a manager in London when I was 24 years old, and there are plenty of people I learnt from. But two people who've inspired me the most. One is my English father, who was captured in Singapore in the Second World War and spent three years in Changi prison of war camp. He didn't teach me about recruitment, but he taught me so much about how you behave with people and how you think about yourself. He taught me to play with a straight bat and that I could succeed without cheating or putting others down. He was very good at conveying that doing the right things is important and how you make people feel is important. I learnt a great deal from him. He died over 30 years ago. When you're 15 to 18, you think your father is out of touch and doesn't know anything. By the time you get to 25 years old, you're shocked to realise how clever he's become, and I'd started to understand what he was talking about. He taught me about resilience and the generation that didn't have much but achieved so much. He provided us with a lot more than he had. But he also taught us to be grateful for what you've got, and you've got to earn what you get, so that was good.

Secondly, Graham Whelan, I wrote a blog years ago called 'The Very Best Recruiter I Have Ever Known', which you can find on my website. He was great because of his humanity. He started recruiting in his early 20s; we started the business together ten years later. He taught me the importance of your reputation, empathy, and delivering on your promises and commitments. He was my boss initially, then we were colleagues, and he reinforced integrity. And he taught me the intrinsic good of what we do and that we actually impact people's lives, and we should never forget that.

The third group is a generation of people I work with now because I'm a board advisor on the Board of 12 recruitment companies, and most of the people I work with are in their 30s or 40s. They started recruitment businesses, built them up to a level, and now they're trying to take it to the next level, and I learn from these people all the time in terms of their work ethic, ambition, coachability, and the success that they have. So, they keep me in tune with the way younger people are thinking.

Contact Greg

Steve: *Greg, if people are trying to find you, where's the best place to come and connect with you?*

Greg: I would be delighted if people connected to me on LinkedIn. Greg Savage should be easy enough to find. I accept connections from anyone in recruitment, HR, or any related area. And you can also read my blog, 'The Savage Truth'. www.gregsavage.com.au – I've been blogging every week for 15 years, so there's a lot of good material there. You can get my books, 'The Savage Truth,' and 'Recruit – The Savage Way'. And there is the comprehensive Savage Recruitment Academy, my online learning platform, all can be found via my website.

Steve: *Greg, it's been an absolute pleasure, thank you.*

Greg's Key Takeaways

- To become a great recruiter, one must understand four main areas: intrinsic attributes, attitude and mindset, learned skills, and the process.
- Intrinsic attributes are the raw, innate abilities one possesses, such as resilience, stamina, work ethic, and empathy, which are crucial in the recruitment industry.
- Attitude and mindset are the long-term view, treating people with integrity, investing in building relationships, and building credibility.
- Learned skills are the specific skills one needs to learn to become a great recruiter, such as sourcing candidates, assessing skills, and building relationships.
- The process involves how recruiters do things, such as using technology, managing time, and managing client expectations.
- Recruitment is hard work, and success requires a nuanced cocktail of different attributes and skills.
- Great recruiters take a long-term view and focus on building relationships, providing excellent customer service, and treating people with integrity.
- The ultimate goal of coaching recruiters is to help them create excellent outcomes.
- Moments of truth in recruitment are those moments where there's an interaction between clients and recruiter or candidate and recruiter, which the recruiter can influence the outcome for the greater good.
- Great recruiters have intrinsic attributes, attitude and mindset, learned skills, and a process that helps them succeed.
- Great recruiters work close to the money, meaning they work on the most fillable jobs, prioritise the jobs where the salaries are appropriate, and work with candidates who can both get job offers and are motivated to accept them.

- Success in recruitment is achieved through high activity and doing high numbers of the right activities.
- The formula for success in recruitment is activity times, quality times target market.
- Recruiters who go from good to great have a mindset of continuous learning, are coachable, and are open to measurement.
- The company's fault for the plateau in a recruiter's performance is that they spend more time training underperforming people, trying to get them to the average level, and less time turning good recruiters into great ones.
- The second reason is the recruiter's fault, which is complacency and hubris, believing they are already great and closed to learning.
- Measurability helps improve a recruiter's performance, which means constant goal-setting, mentoring, and giving people nano degrees (90-100-day self-taught subjects).
- Recruitment companies fail their high performers by leaving them alone instead of helping them go from good to great or great to exceptional through a plan, resulting in billings plateauing or sometimes going backwards.
- Recruitment companies leave their top, highest billers alone because most owners are not good business managers and leaders, and they bow down to high billings and allow high-billing recruiters to get away with a lot of things.

Contact Greg

The Savage Recruitment Academy www.gregsavage.com.au
The Savage Truth Blog www.gregsavage.com.au/the-savage-truth/
The Savage Truth. Book.
www.gregsavage.com.au/the-savage-truth-book/
Recruit – The Savage Way. Book
www.gregsavage.com.au/recruit-the-savage-way/
LinkedIn linkedin.com/in/gregpsavage

Greg's Q&A

What's your version of success?

In personal relationships, family, friends, and colleagues, the measure of success is that, in the end, with the benefit of hindsight, they might say that you 'gave at least as much as you took'. That is a success.

In business, it's just getting to the point that your business and career achievements allow you to have more *choices in life*. Being able to decide what you do, when you do it, and who you do it with is true success.

What's your favourite quote?

"Most people are other people. Their thoughts are someone else's opinions, their lives a mimicry, their passions a quotation." – Oscar Wilde

I see very little use for quotations. Especially those spouted on social media as though they are helpful to anyone and meant to be 'deep' and motivating. Don't give me quotes. Instead, tell me *what you know or think*.

What advice would you give your younger self?

Be kinder. Be 'slower to understand'. Make fewer assumptions. Listen much more. Understand that everyone is fighting a hard fight.

What is the best investment you have made, and why?

It was helping other people, even as my own star rose. Giving my time and expertise. I didn't do it for personal benefit, but over time it has reaped more than I could have imagined— friendships, loyalty, business partners, advocates, networks, referrals, and gratitude.

Investment in a financial sense? Backing several founders of recruitment businesses (*including myself a few times*) who created companies of value.

What's your go-to productivity trick?

Step back from the coal face. Evaluate your priorities. 'Triage' the work. Be clear on critical outcomes. Focus on these.

Also, it looks impossibly vast and challenging when faced with an immense task, like writing a report, a business plan, preparing a speech, or even writing a book. Just start. Once you start, you are 'in it'; once you are in it, you are nearing the end with every step you take.

If you could write a book about your life, what would the title be and why?

I did. It's called 'The Savage Truth'. What else could it be called?

What's one thing you're learning now, and why is it important?

To cut back on work. Take on fewer clients and projects. Wean myself off engagements that are no longer right for all parties. It is important because I should stick to my mantra outlined in question 1 above. *Work with people you like on projects you are passionate about.* But also, I am 64. So, I need to transition from working at the same pace I have for 45 years to a little more balanced one.

I am also consciously working on learning more about SAAS business models because I am on the Board of a SAAS business. Also, I have launched the Savage Recruitment Academy, a subscription learning platform. It has surprised me with its success, and I need to understand this niche much better because I have another real business on my hands. I feel slightly out of my depth on the tech and the marketing.

Who would you choose if you could trade places with anyone for a day?

I can honestly say I have never even thought of being anyone else. Not that my life, or me, is perfect. Very far from it. But surely, we all know everyone's life is not what it seems from the outside. I wonder how many little girls wished they were Princess Diana back in the day. Do you think that would have been a good swap?

CHAPTER FOUR

Jamie York

(Property)

About Jamie

J amie York is a property investor, speaker, and entrepreneur and is the Managing Director of Aspire Property Group; a property investment consultancy based in Yorkshire.

Jamie has been investing in property for the best part of a decade, starting his property portfolio at just 19 years old, with his first investment in Burnley. However, with no experience in the property space at that time, that first property for Jamie wasn't exactly smooth sailing. To give you a small taster of how Jamie's first investment went, it is worth noting that his new kitchen for the property refurb ended up in the neighbour's house, not in his investment property! Pipes from under the floorboards were stolen, and did the figures stack up? Well, not really. If you ever meet Jamie, no doubt he will explain all, and expand on the challenges of that first deal for you and give you your first lesson: consume as much knowledge as you can and go into your first deal armed with that information.

Knowing property investment, done right, could be life-changing, Jamie decided he needed to up his understanding of property investment.

After growing his property knowledge and getting an education in the industry, Jamie moved from Kent to Yorkshire – settling in Leeds, where he began working as a head-hunter. On evenings and weekends, he hustled hard on his property business, building up some rent-to-rent properties and dealing with other investors. After a few years, Jamie sold his rent to rents and knuckled down on the deal sourcing, combining that with investing himself. Over the next few years, Jamie grew his property portfolio, becoming a millionaire at 25 years old, and grew his deal-sourcing business to become Aspire Property Group as it is known today.

After his success in the property investment space over the years, Jamie has created more time and freedom, enabling him to think about what he wanted from life. Property had such a huge impact on him. He didn't come from a wealthy background and hadn't had connections in the industry before he started. Because of the impactful change that had taken place, Jamie wanted to help as many others realise their potential. He wanted to simplify property to make it as accessible as possible to everyone. He launched his education company in 2020 and a YouTube channel the following year to add value to as many people as possible and help them change their mindset and their future. This continues to be one of Jamie's core focuses' as he continues his property investment journey.

In Jamie's own words:

Motivation

Steve: *I started my property journey in 2016, and that was the first time I saw you talk. Of all speakers at the event, you were the one that grabbed my attention. I don't know what it was, whether it was the story, the setup or your personality, but something about you was engaging.*

You pushed me to take that first jump into property, which can be really scary. Seeing as you inspired me, could you give an overview of what inspires and motivates you?

Jamie: That is great to hear! For me, it's the challenge of it. I know that is such a blasé thing to say, but actually, when you start making money, when you start developing yourself, and especially when you get some passive income as well, that looks after all of your financial needs, that's when you truly work out whether you're a businessperson or an entrepreneur. There is a big divide between the two. If you're a business person, and it's not just that entrepreneurial spirit, then there's no need to take on more and stress yourself out. Because, let's face it, being an entrepreneur is stressful as hell. I think being an entrepreneur is linked to embracing that challenge. A challenge must be your oxygen in life, almost like you can't live without it. I've really recognised some behaviours in myself. On my days off, unless they are planned days off and I have something to do, I literally shut down. I'm a fish out of water because this is my life, and when I am not overcoming a challenge, I'm almost looking around like, 'What's next?'

People talk about work-life balance – it's absolute bullshit. I don't buy into it at all. Maybe that works for some people, but I call it a blended lifestyle. The main difference is I love work, so I don't need to go on a holiday to get away from it, but I love holidays that combine relaxing by a pool, jumping on a webinar, followed by a hike – you can have it all!

If I went to the pub, like everyone else, and I was having a couple of drinks, my idea of fun is to go into the pub with people who want to talk shop, talk about money, and building businesses. Talk about the problems and the solutions in business. That, for me, is the way my world goes around. I have no interest in holidays where I switch off for a few weeks because there's no such thing for me.

I wake up, and most days, I'm pretty much into that growth mindset. Thinking about strategy and solutions. I live and breathe it, and I'm genuinely passionate about it. I absolutely love problems, and as an entrepreneur, that's a mindset shift. In the start, problems are bad, right? It's like a relationship with no passion. You're going to have arguments every now and then. But if you have a relationship with nothing, no passion, and no engagement, it will get boring after a while. It's the same with life. I think entrepreneurs are solution providers, so if you can positively seek problems (I'm not talking about people with these horrible habits that are degrading and negative), but have positive engagement with these problems with a solution focus, it makes the business world so much more interesting. For me, that is the real mindset of an entrepreneur, and that passion and love for what I do keeps me motivated.

On Staying Motivated

Having moments where you feel unmotivated needs to be more normalised in the world of entrepreneurs. Successful entrepreneurs genuinely are another level of motivation, and the work they put in is how they get their outcomes. But it doesn't mean you are never unmotivated – you will have those days, I certainly do, and probably far more regularly than what most people realise. I get demotivated monthly, if not weekly! This morning, in fact, I woke up, and I was meeting somebody at 6:30 am for a swim, and I just thought, "fu*k that. Why? I've just got no time for that, and I'm knackered". It was freezing cold outside, and I was well and truly wrapped up in bed – that kind of wrapped up where you feel like you couldn't be any more comfortable and have no intention of moving anytime soon. I'm human, and that's the thing that people need to connect themselves with. We are human; even the absolute machines of the world need to crash in bed and have a takeaway once in a while. I'm no different. I fu*k up all the time. I get emotional. I cry. I hate life. Sometimes I wake up and wonder, 'Is this all worth it?' I think from an external perspective, it's just not as obvious that the lack of motivation exists because it seems like I'm constantly: go, go, go, and will probably be more 'go, go, go' than the average person.

People say I'm always at 110%, but I have high intentions around things which is probably why it seems like there is that high level of motivation consistently. I think having intent is key to staying motivated. I'm present in the moment and minimise distractions as much as possible. Like now, things are going on around me; somebody is going in and out of the kitchen grabbing coffees, I can hear some conversations in the background, and my phone is next to me. But my phone is on silent, and it's in sleep mode. The reason for that is so I can be committed to this moment in time.

To the outside world, it might seem that I'm waking up at three in the morning and going to sleep at two in the morning, but I'm getting my hours of sleep in. I work out at least four times a week because I know when I don't, I'm less motivated with everything I do. I get my steps in on calls because I feel lethargic if I don't walk. I watch my diet but still have a sticky toffee pudding at the pub – that I'm able to talk about business – because I enjoy food, but if I eat shit all the time, I feel unmotivated, but if I restrict myself to a diet of lettuce and celery. I feel shit. It's about a blended life. Having a blended life enables me to stay motivated. The things I do are varied, I'm not restricting myself, and I have balance – which all ties into staying motivated.

One thing I have tried that works for me is something that I call the 1–3–5 method. The idea is that every single day, and I mean every day, Monday to Sunday, there is one thing I absolutely must do, three things I really should get done, and five things that I could do. What we tend to do in life is start with those five things you could do; it's not to say they're not high value, maybe things like sending an email out to your list if you're a solo entrepreneur, but an email won't be the most important thing you must do. Emails are positive procrastination, making you feel like you are doing a lot, but really you are not doing those high-value, impactful tasks.

The great thing about watching Netflix is that you're f**king around, and you know it – so you can get out of it what you intend to: to switch off. Whereas when you're sending emails and replying to emails, you convince yourself that they've got to get answers from you. No, they don't. Nobody cares about emails. No email was ever urgent; people call if it's really urgent. So, the '1 – 3 – 5 method' is one thing I must do, three things I should do, and five things I could do. It allows me to be an absolute machine. And if you can mix that in with something like the Pomodoro technique, which combines set work times with regular breaks, that enables you to stay motivated when you are doing a task. If you can do four or five rounds of that, you will do in a day what you usually get done in a week. It's so powerful because it is that combination of balance that is sustainable.

But remember what I said at the beginning, there are days that I wake up, maybe a couple of times a month, and I just can't be bothered. Or I'll be knackered as I couldn't sleep the night before because my thoughts are racing. On those days, it is important to accept that you are human, we all have them, and then the next important factor is to focus on the one thing I MUST do. That's the one from the 1 – 3 – 5 method. It is the most important thing on your daily list. So, on those days when you have no motivation, don't worry about the full list; focus on just that one thing. That one thing is not necessarily the longest task; it's the most important, highest value and urgent task. It might take me half an hour to do, or it might take me three hours to do; it doesn't matter – I get up and get it done, no matter what. And I like doing it because on those crap days, once I've got out of bed and done that one task that is really high value, I'd say 80% of the time, I feel ready to smash the rest of the day, pushing through that first task is the motivator I need.

Then I'll have my coffee, I'll be raring to go, and I'll dominate. I usually like to get in the office between 7:00 and 8:00 am to beat the crowd and get some tasks smashed out before everyone else rocks up. 20% of the time, I get back into bed after my one 'MUST do' task, and I'm not having any of it. I get back into bed; I'll chill out, eat sh*t, and watch Netflix. But I still did one genuinely high-value task towards my growth.

People are obsessed with the huge growth of the 1%. But actually, think of it like a marathon. A marathon is only a series of steps. That's all it is.

It's only when you put the time barrier on it and say you need to run it in a set time that it becomes a much harder competition. But actually, a marathon can be completed with far more ease if each day you train for it and on the day of the marathon itself, remember, it's just one step at a time. If you think about the basics, the same as business, same as life, same as growth, same as happiness, same as everything, it's just one step forward. And so, the absolute minimum that I will allow myself each day is one tiny step forward. Once I've done that, I'm progressing. I never, ever, ever take a step back. No days are wasted, not one in the year, because an inch is an inch, and that's how you stay motivated.

On The Journey to Success

Steve: *I firmly believe in the 1% and the Compound Effect by Darren Hardy – the thought process of making that one extra sales call on pushing for that one extra interview. The impact over the years is so important. Most people, however, want to rush to the finish line or make a massive move that makes them stand out. I've made a career out of being that quiet, unassuming consultant at the back of the room that doesn't ring the bell when he makes a placement because the job isn't done yet. I want to be the person that creeps up behind, so to speak (not in a weird way!).*

Jamie: Absolutely. I recently did a course by Matt D'Avella. His brand is called the Slow Growth Academy. And one thing connected with me when he said, "Do you know people would be far more successful and happier if they changed the three-week mindset into a three-year mindset?"

He explains that if you're trying to get rich quickly, you can guarantee to make someone else rich and probably make yourself poor in the meantime. Many trainers tell you that you can quit your job next month and get rich. Don't listen to them; you can't – it's not reality! Instead, if you come into this game and identify your three-year goals, you can suddenly achieve a lot more. If you had a five-year target to be a millionaire, I believe that person more and have confidence in their ability to be a success than somebody saying, "I want to make £50,000 in my first six months."

People think £50,000 is easy, but it's not. The first £50,000 in business is so difficult. It's the hardest money I think you'll ever make. And once you break past that, it's just exponential. If you look at any progress curve, take YouTube growth, for example; my financial net worth growth can go up £100k a month. A lot of people will say, "That's amazing", But remember, it's taken me ten years to get to that higher growth. I didn't wake up yesterday with my property investment knowledge and launch my YouTube channel. That knowledge has been years in the making. Ask anyone if they would put in 10 years to get to that point, and the answer is always 'yes'. So, it's just a matter of taking those small steps every day.

What are you doing on a daily basis?
What are you putting in your mind?
What are you putting in your body?
Who are you surrounding yourself with?

Ask yourself these questions, as these are the inputs. Things like wealth, growth and knowledge are the long-term outcomes of the consistency you create.

On Accountability

Steve: *I remember a few years ago, I had put forward a tender that needed to be finished. I was relying on somebody else to complete the tender, and they missed the deadline, and as a result, we lost the tender. I lost my rag and stormed into the director's office, slamming the door open. The director explained to me that it was, in fact, my fault. He said, "Your client, your tender. Why haven't you managed it better? Why didn't you manage the process? It's 100% your fault." I got a huge tearing down, but I deserved it because he was right – I didn't manage* the tender properly. From that day, my thought process has been that everything is 100% my fault, good and bad. I sink and swim by the decisions I make. Sure, I will make mistakes, but I'm not frightened by them. I can stand by and say I made that decision because of x, y, or z. We live in a blame culture where we'll always shout that it's someone else's fault for not achieving or "I didn't get picked because of x, y or z". We need to take responsibility and make things work for ourselves.

Jamie: Words are so powerful. What's the difference between who's taking the blame and who's accountable? They're very similar things! What makes somebody influential? And what makes somebody manipulative? They are very similar things, just with a different tonality and insinuation. Accepting responsibility definitely creates quicker growth in an individual. You analyse your own actions far more. As you say, even if you don't believe a mistake is a mistake, or created by your decision, if you have the mindset where you do check in with yourself and hold yourself accountable, you are far more likely to be able to explain your reasoning behind an action whilst not creating blame.

As a business owner, you're accountable for everything. If you have staff making mistakes, you need to look at your training. Is it really good enough? If you have staff that are consistently late, you need to look at your policies because you are normalising that behaviour if you take no action. It's a trickle-down impact, for sure.

Making mistakes really does teach you and creates strong and lasting lessons as long as you know to reflect on them and consider your role within them rather than externally looking to find a reason for them or blame them.

What drives you?

It goes back to that age-old argument of nature versus nurture. If you look at the nurture of my environment, there were probably some predictable moments in my life that created the drive I have had for as long as I can remember. I was a relatively bright kid, did the 11+, and passed; I got into a good school that was third in the country for results at the time. I was surrounded by many people who had gone to private schools. I ended up surrounded by wealthy families. They had money behind them and a very different life from the one I had experienced. I grew up in Dartford, in Temple Hill. I never felt poor at all because I was happy with what I had and knew no different, but suddenly, as I entered secondary school, I witnessed a whole new level of life. People were talking about their yearly skiing trip, and I sat there thinking, "That is so posh!". We went to Haven Holiday Park growing up, which I have to say was brilliant!

The more I got to know people who had that wealth and hadn't experienced anything outside of it, I realised the money didn't make them happier, but they also had no comparison; that level of wealth was all they knew, so there wasn't necessarily the same drive there to create more wealth. Although I don't believe money makes you happy, I think the absence of money can cause a lot of pain and strife. My dad passed away when I was 13, and that was quite a pivotal moment when it came to considering where my drive comes from. I was about to turn 14; he died in September, and my birthday was in November. He was 38 years old, seven years older than I am now, which is way too young. It gave me real appreciation. I heard a line around that time: "Everybody dies, but not many truly live". And I thought, "Okay, if I do die at 38, that will be sh*t, and I don't want that to happen, but if I do, have I lived?"

I think the combination of not having money growing up, being catapulted into a world where people had always had money, and then the sudden loss of my dad made me realise how quickly things can change. It also made me want to keep my family safe, and that started me on a shift in mindset to provide for them and make sure they always had what they needed and could make the most of their lives. When you really embrace the fragility of life and how quickly it can be taken away from you, it gives you appreciation.

There will be somebody in most of our lives that we are close to, and at some point, they pass away, and it gets us thinking. It makes us reflect. You might think, "Life is short; I just saw them last week." But, it can take something negative to actually end up having a positive shift in an individual's mindset. Don't get me wrong, I'd give everything to have my dad back for a day, but it really set me on a path where I became more driven and wanted to seek out my purpose.

This takes us to the nature part of nature versus nurture. I've always been a bit of a hustler – selling sausage rolls at school and fixing mini diggers at 13 for extra cash. I've always been pretty good with my hands, but never been at the top of the class in anything, but I have been smart enough to think of an idea and know I need to take action – sometimes taking too much action and not giving myself space to think!

I am definitely driven by money; I love money and don't see it as negative. It's a vehicle. If you're a philanthropist and you're a multi, multi, multi, multi-millionaire, you can give more away. If you're a prick, then you're going to be more of a prick. Money doesn't do anything. People say money changes people, but it doesn't – it reveals who you are. I am driven by money, but I want to make meaningful changes. And maybe this is my ego because every selfless act is arguably selfish. By the time I die, whether that is 38 years old, 58 years old or 98 years old, I want to have impacted people's lives so I am remembered for the positive changes I have made, and that is a real driver for me.

I set up my education company to teach people how to invest in property and change their lives. Set up my YouTube channel because I feel so passionate about personal development, and I know not everyone has access to funds instantly to be able to pay for structured education, but that shouldn't mean people can't start learning – and I want the property to be as accessible as possible for people. Actions within my business are all related to personal passions, and it is very easy to be driven when you are passionate.

On Sales

Steve: *I've been in recruitment for 18 years, and the average lifespan of a recruitment consultant is six months across any sector and industry. I get the fact it's difficult as there are lots of KPIs, internal and external. You're dealing with people who can let you down at the best and worst moments, and it's tough psychologically from a sales perspective. I find that the willingness to go at it and have that continued belief is a rarity.*

Jamie: I love selling. I see a sales role as close to owning a business as you can get. Because as a salesperson, you own your position, and you're almost a business entity within yourself. I love that responsibility; I've always loved that pressure. I'd hate to work in a salary position; my personality couldn't hack it. I don't like the idea that you can get better results in a position but not necessarily more money or have to wait for a promotion for that to be recognised. Whereas in sales, if you want to stay in the office and do that extra phone call, over time, that's going to pay £ 1,000's. And it's exponential, so if you give it your all and throw yourself at it continuously in the right direction, with the right education and support mechanisms, you will be paid and rewarded very well. In the same way, if you're flaky, you'll lose it all.

I have learnt over the years to be an incredible salesperson; you need to listen and understand what somebody needs. And sometimes, you will know what they need more than they know. But, you also need to recognise when you are not going to be able to provide the best solution for them, and communicate that and maybe even point them in the right direction.

On Winning And Losing

Winners win, and losers lose. It sounds harsh, but it's true, and we all have the potential to be winners or losers; it comes down to your mindset. When I was in trading, and we had a big loss, I'd pack up for the day and come back the next day with a new mindset, ready to hit the day hard again. If I saw the day out, my behaviour would represent a spike in negative emotion, and my approach to the rest of the day would be negative, so if you can step away and take a breather, why not do that? If I carried on, there is a high chance I would make loss after loss for the remainder of the day because that is where your head is at – you're not in the game! You react emotionally when you get those sudden losses.

Often, when you start down that track of negativity – where there might be a catalyst, but you don't take that step back, you fuel the negativity yourself. Like 'the glass is half empty', it is the way you look at everything. You don't see the opportunities because you don't allow yourself to.

On Inspiration

Jamie: My biggest inspirations? First of all, I have to start with my mum. She was a single mum with four kids, my dad left when I was three months old, and she balanced looking after us with work. And trust me, I was no angel, so it wasn't an easy task. She is the matriarch of my family; everyone goes to my mum for life advice. She is emotionally in tune with others, understands people, and reads people extremely well. She just has the answers and applies logic to make you think differently about a situation, which has helped me repeatedly throughout life. She's also incredibly good at managing money. My dad was very good at making money – he was just sh*t at managing it effectively and used to spend it all. So, in my early years, I got the best of both worlds. I saw how my dad hustled hard and how my mum managed her finances. It embraced these learnings and then, over the years, learnt how to multiply the money. This is the 3 M's: Making Money, Managing Money and Multiplying Money.

Another inspiration was a poem that my dad gave me for my birthday one year. It's a poem called 'If' by Rudyard Kipling.

If you can talk with crowds and keep your virtue,
Or walk with Kings—nor lose the common touch,
If neither foes nor loving friends can hurt you,
If all men count with you, but none too much;
If you can fill the unforgiving minute
With sixty seconds' worth of distance run,
Yours is the Earth and everything that's in it,
And—what is more—you'll be a Man, my son!

It was such a sentimental gift, connecting me to what's possible and important. It's about not getting upset about the trivial things in life and focusing on the things that are important. It brings me back to the idea of creating a life of balance.

The final person I will mention that has inspired me is a guy called Dean Graziosi. He has done a lot with Tony Robbins, and his mindset really got me hooked. I remember him saying, "One day, you're going to see me on stage with Tony Robbins". Tony Robbins is like The Godfather, right? And I remember thinking that is a big call to make.

Yet, he was so anchored to that, and now he runs programs with Tony Robbins. That sort of person blows me away, who can look and see ten years ahead and work to make their goal a reality, even if it seems so unattainable, even if there is doubt from others. There are controllable and uncontrollable things, and you need to learn from the uncontrollable things in your life. Do what you can to overcome them and control the controllable. Say 'this is me' in 10 years' time, and as soon as you can fully embrace that and decide, "Actually, I am the writer of my story, and my future is completely within my control", you're in control. And that's why I connect so much with Dean Graziosi.

Inspiration can be drawn from so many different places. Although these that I have mentioned are definitely at the forefront of my mind when I think about inspiration, I am definitely inspired by a whole host of people in different ways. Places can inspire me; experiences inspire

me. I think inspiration is all about something fuelling a passi‹
you and just giving you that nudge you need to take action.

One single piece of advice

Either give up quickly or never give up. You may have seen that image
of the person mining consistently, and then he gives up, and he's only
three inches away from the diamond mine, but because he didn't
realise that, he just stopped. There are multiple questions that stop
people from progressing – what if you're not on the right path? You can
move really quickly, but what if it's in the wrong direction?

It is important to think strategically about your direction and throw
yourself 100% at it. Life is too short to do something you aren't
enthusiastic about, so if you're not feeling it, stop trying to force
yourself to do it. You won't put in the effort you need to be successful
if you don't feel passionate about what you're doing. So, give up. Give
up, and find that 'thing' that creates passion and that desire to keep on
pushing. People find what they are great at by finding a load of things
that they are shit at.

People find things they are passionate about by finding things they're
not passionate about. People succeed by failing a lot of times and
learning from those failures. So, give up quickly if it's not for you, and
invest your time into something new. It's okay to reinvent yourself.

Jamie York in Summary

- Being an entrepreneur is linked to embracing challenges.
- Entrepreneurs love problems and are solution providers and
  positively seek problems with a solution focus.

- Even the most driven people get demotivated, so it's important to remember that everyone is human and needs rest.
- Use the 1 – 3 – 5 method to stay productive every day, which involves doing one must-do, three should-do, and five could-do tasks each day.
- Avoid positive procrastination by focusing on high-value tasks instead of tasks you could do.
- A blended life is essential for entrepreneurs; work-life balance is not always achievable.
- Change your three-week mindset into a three-year mindset. Identify your three-year goals instead of trying to get rich quickly.
- Take small steps every day towards achieving your goals.
- Focus on what you do daily, what you put in your mind and body, and who you surround yourself with.
- Take accountability for everything, good or bad. Everything is 100% your fault, and you sink or swim by your own decisions.
- Avoid blaming others for your failures or shortcomings. Instead, take responsibility and make things work for yourself.
- Money doesn't make you happy, but the absence of it can cause pain.
- Appreciate the value of time and try not to waste it. Live life to the fullest.

Contact Jamie

www.jamieyork.co.uk
hello@jamieyork.com
Insta – @jamieyorkofficial
YouTube – @jamieyork

Jamie's Q&A

What's your version of success?

Success for me is having 'success' in all areas of my life. I don't believe I'll be insane at business, be an Olympic athlete, and be an award-winning actor. But I believe I can be successful in business, health and fitness, personal life, and the person I want to be.

When I am working at the best version of myself, I can create financial success and knowledge wealth, combining the two to enable me to have freedom and choice in my life, so I can then spend my time in the areas I get true value from – inspiring others to make changes to their lives and reach their full potential.

Top three books to read or listen to?

The Richest Man In Babylon – George S Clason
Psycho-Cybernetics – Maxwell Maltz
Ego Is The Enemy – Ryan Holiday

What's your favourite quote?

You must be the change you wish to see in the world – Gandhi.

What advice would you give your younger self?

Do not neglect yourself by looking after everyone around you to the extent that you are not understanding or registering your own emotions.

What is the best investment you have made, and why?

Investing in myself – building up my knowledge, and progressing my self-development means I can turn up as my best self each day. So, the application of that to my business means I'm developing exponentially. Why learn from my own lessons and mistakes when I can invest in mentoring and learn from theirs?

What's your go-to productivity trick?

Set constraints around everything; it's time management on steroids. For example, don't have a to-do list; instead, put it into your calendar and challenge yourself to get the task done within the time constraint; you'll thank me for it. Think of that essay you had three months to do at school and pulled it out of the bag the night before. Structure creates habits!

If you could write a book about your life, what would the title be and why?

Lucky Me – I've always been labelled as 'lucky' by people around me, and I think it's important to talk about luck not really existing. Everyone goes through challenges in life, and because, as humans, we focus so much on our own world, we often feel far less 'lucky' than the people around us. But we are just not living their lives, so we couldn't compare. Success takes time, and overcoming challenges takes time – these things do not just happen overnight, and there isn't a quick route to becoming successful, so dissecting the ups and downs of my own life and talking more about this would hopefully benefit other people.

What's one thing you're learning now, and why is it important?

I am putting a lot of time into learning how to be the best leader. There are many moving parts in play when you are leading. First, there needs to be a strength in your communication. That communication needs to be adaptable depending on how best the receiver learns or understands. You need to ensure your passion is apparent and your vision is clear. It's about looking at the bigger picture to ensure the business moves forward and the team as individuals grow to be the best versions of themselves.

Who would you choose if you could trade places with anyone for a day?

My business head immediately jumps to someone like Tony Robbins, who has always inspired me, and I think learning from his journey would have a real impact.

CHAPTER FIVE

Jeremy Lazarus

(Money)

About Jeremy

Jeremy is an accredited master executive coach, an ILM-approved coach trainer and a certified NLP master trainer. Before becoming a Business Coach and Trainer in 1999, Jeremy had 18 years experience as a senior finance professional and management consultant, including being the finance director of YO! Sushi; he is a qualified accountant and a qualified corporate treasurer. Jeremy's clients include blue chip SMEs, several NHS Trusts, charities and elite athletes; a guest lecturer at UK universities, he has written four best-selling books and has just started writing his fifth—also an ex-semi-professional footballer and a very keen tennis player.

In Jeremy's words:

The mindset for success.

Jeremy: The key factor distinguishing successful people from the rest is their mindset. Some people naturally have a positive mindset for success, whereas others may feel they need to work to develop it. There are five key beliefs in the mindset for success, and I will also cover six principles for success and give evidence for this. And then I want to talk about the one thing I've been training people for over 23 years, a topic that is the most useful and valuable five or 10 minutes of education people ever have in their whole life. I know that is a big statement, and I don't want you to believe it just yet; I'll highlight it when we get to it, and then you can decide how relevant it is.

Whether the topic is money, sports, business, or life, generally, people with a positive mindset can achieve way more than someone who doesn't. And you can work at it; people aren't just born with it. It's not genetic. Any skill or any attribute can be developed. You'll find people from the most challenging backgrounds who do incredibly well for themselves. And then other people are born with many advantages who don't do as well for themselves. Some say, "Oh, it's easy for you because you're this and that. It's difficult for him because he's that!" I don't accept that. People can choose the kind of life they want to have.

Self-awareness is essential, but it's more than that. The most significant factor is desire. In his book, Think and Grow Rich, Napoleon Hill says that having a compelling desire, an overriding goal, and an aim is key. If people want something badly enough, even if they don't yet have the skills or the abilities, they'll somehow find a way to do it.

That's why the mindset for success is so important. It's about beliefs.

Key Beliefs

I call it the mindset of success and the principles for success. It helps you to group them. Here are five of what I consider to be the mindset for success elements. These are beliefs, not truths. It's not like I'm preaching the gospel or anything like that; these are just helpful beliefs to have.

1. Have 'respect' for other people's points of view and their individuality. That doesn't mean you like or agree with them. In business or life, if you feel someone respects where you're coming from, you're more likely to engage with them, even if you disagree. In his book, The Seven Habits of Highly Effective People, Stephen Covey, one of the seven habits is to 'seek first to understand and then be understood', which is similar to having 'respect' for someone else's perspective.

2. There's no failure, just feedback, learnings and outcomes. I have many examples that resonate with me. When doing the research on the first book I wrote (about NLP and sport), I read several books and articles. Billie Jean King, the tennis champion; Sebastian Coe, the Olympic gold medallist; and Roger Black, the 400-metre champion, all said that, while it took them a while to realise it, there was no failure, just feedback. Remember, this is about mindset. If there was ever a person who hated losing, it was Billie Jean King, and yet she realised that when she lost a match, whilst she wasn't happy about it, it was feedback that she had to do something differently next time. It's just a learning experience, and I suggest that this is one of the things that helped keep her at the top of the game for such a long time. A workplace example to illustrate the 'no failure, only feedback, learnings and outcomes' concept is Thomas Edison, the scientist who created the light bulb. Allegedly it took him 10,000 times to make the light bulb. People asked Dr Edison, "What was it like having failed 10,000 times?"

"I didn't fail," he said. "I successfully found 10,000 ways that didn't work."

3. The more flexible people can be, the better their chances of success. Staying with the Thomas Edison example. Presumably, each subsequent experiment was different from the previous ones.

   Albert Einstein once said, "The definition of insanity is doing the same thing over and over and expecting different results." So be prepared to be flexible in what you're doing and how you're doing it.

4. We all have the resources we need to succeed and achieve our desired outcome. And when I say resources, I mean internal resources, such as determination, resilience, ability to learn and compassion. In my training courses, when I see some people question this point, I tell them, "Think about a time in your past, where you had a real challenge, where you were really up against it, and you had to dig deep; somehow you found it inside you to overcome that." Every person can relate to that. So, to succeed, it's important to recognise that we can go further than we think. Recognise that the 'fall downs' are not failures as long as you get yourself back up again. Imagine a toddler starting to walk, they don't know failure, so when they fall, they get up and do it again.

Steve: And that's the innocence of it all – the fact that kids keep going. As adults, or as we grow up, sometimes we put hurdles in place that protect us because we fear the failure of falling.

Jeremy: Yes, we put hurdles in the way – it's not other people putting hurdles there.

5. The fifth point of success is that if someone in a similar situation can do something, so can you. Of course, apply

common sense. So just because Usain Bolt can run 100 metres in 9.58 seconds doesn't mean we all can! But I know many of your listeners will be recruiters and aim to have a successful recruitment consultancy with 50 team members turning over £10,000,000, for example. Some people started from nothing and have built a recruitment business to that size, so if someone else can do it, then so can you if you want it badly enough. When I coach people, I often ask about a specific goal they want to achieve. I then ask them who they know who's done that. Then I suggest they find out how they did it by reading up or asking. If you discover the approach that someone else has, it will help you reach your goal, and even if you don't have access to them, just the fact that they've done it, will give you the belief that it is possible.

Steve: *Quite often, we think that we've got to reinvent the wheel, do things our own way, and that we don't need to ask anyone else. But the more logical thing to do is to go and sit with someone that's done it so you don't make all the mistakes, but people hardly ever do that.*

Jeremy: Exactly, for the sake of a bit of research and a few conversations, the worst that can happen is you waste a couple of hours, and the best thing that can happen is that you could save yourself weeks, months, or years going down the wrong tunnels.

Steve: *It was 2016 when I started surrounding myself with other people that have been through the proprty process. The moment I opened up the idea of having mentors and coaches and surrounding myself with people that have done what I'm looking to do, the process became more enjoyable, and less risky, because you can ask questions when you've got doubts, fears or worries. So that's one of the benefits of having a coach and a mentor.*

The Principles of Success

Jeremy: This is a series of beliefs and a topic that has been in the field of NLP for several years. In 2011, I did my master's degree, and my dissertation was on mental strength in elite professional goalkeepers. I played in goal semi-professionally, and I was interested in mindset. I interviewed Premier League and Championship goalkeepers and Premier League goalkeeping coaches. If you are not interested in football, still take heed, as I believe we can always learn from people at the top of their respective fields.

I did 15 hours of interviews with 130,000 words of transcript, and the model I'm about to explain jumped out at me. Even though they didn't know about NLP or this model, these athletes were doing it naturally. Let me take you through the six points.

1. Know your desired outcome or your goal before you start. Whether that's in your life generally or whether it's a specific activity, like a negotiation – know what you want from the negotiation.

2. Take action. It's one thing to know what you want; it's another to do something about it.

3. Gather information. Say you're in a meeting; you will observe, notice the body language, listen to the voice, and take feedback about what's happening.

4. Be flexible. If what you're doing is working, then great, but if it's not, be prepared to adapt or flex what you're doing.

5. Build and maintain good relationships. Even if you disagree with someone, resolving it or getting to a mutually acceptable outcome is usually useful.

6. Have a positive mental attitude, which is an overarching point.

Cause and Effect

There's an underlying 'cause' for every 'effect', and we can extend this principle to humans. So, if you think about mindset, we can be 'At Cause' or 'At Effect'. What do these two terms mean? If someone's 'At Effect', they have the mentality of "the causes for my problems are all out there somewhere, and I'm at the effect of those causes". For example (and this is a fictional example), "Because I went to a really bad school. I haven't got any qualifications. Because my teachers told me I was stupid. I'm not doing very well in my life. Because I came from an awful background, all my relationships are bad. Because the economy's a bit dodgy, my business isn't going well." What we tend to find with people with that mindset is they complain a lot, make excuses, blame others, have a negative 'can't do' attitude, and have a victim mentality. We've all met people like that.

The other side of the equation is someone with the mindset that they can do something about it. For example, "I went to a really bad school, I didn't get any qualifications, so I went to the Open University to get my degree that way." Or "I'm going to succeed without qualifications." "I had a bad upbringing, but I'm going to get some counselling; I'm going to read a lot of books and make sure that my kids never have to put up with what I had to put up with." "The economy isn't good, but there are people still recruiting. How can I be flexible and adapt to meet the needs of the people out there?"

People with the latter mindset tend to get better results because they take 100% responsibility for the results they produce in their life, and if nothing else, they can choose how they respond. So even if the deal you thought was signed and sealed turns out not to be signed and sealed, you can choose how you respond to that situation.

I want to talk about Viktor Frankl, an Austrian Jew, a qualified doctor, and a qualified psychotherapist. He was captured in the Second World War and put in a concentration camp. He managed to survive it and wrote a book called *Man's Search for Meaning*. It's not a big book, but it's an important book. He told a particular story of a prisoner who was down to his last piece of bread, and this prisoner gave his last piece of bread to a fellow prisoner in an even worse position. Let's reflect on that. Imagine you're working for 15 hours a day in appalling conditions, and you could be in a gas chamber any minute, or they could be doing medical experiments on you without anaesthetic at any minute. You are absolutely starving, yet you give your last piece of bread to someone in an even worse position. Frankl looked at this and asked himself what would cause this prisoner, who was starving, to give his last piece of bread to someone else in an even worse position. He realised that everything could be taken away from us, and in the concentration camps, pretty much everything was taken away, including the gold and silver fillings in their teeth. Everything can be taken away from people, except one thing, which Frankl called 'the last of the human freedoms', which is 'to choose our own response to any given set of circumstances, to choose our own way'.

No matter how bad things are business-wise, I'm going to suggest that relatively few people have experienced what Frankl did. So, we have a choice; I know life has challenges. I get it; the market may be difficult, or you may have had a bad few months, or deals have yet to land, but we have a choice. So, if people hang on to that, know where they want to go and are totally committed to their goal, that will make the difference. And even if people don't yet have the capabilities to do something, if their mindset and desire are strong enough, they will go and learn; they'll go on courses, they will read books, they'll soak up information, they will do whatever it takes to achieve their goal. And that's what it's about.

Steve: *I love that. What a statement! I think we should all consider how we can apply that to our lives.*

NLP

Jeremy: NLP stands for Neuro-Linguistic Programming, which is a mouthful, so let me explain what it's about. So, neurolinguistics uses the language of your mind to change the programs or patterns of behaviour. We've all got patterns of behaviour, and some people will metaphorically ride a bike or fall off and think, "I can't do it again". Others will fall off and get back on. So, we've got different patterns of behaviour. So, to summarise NLP. It's a series of tools and techniques with three key benefits. The first benefit is improved communication. So, in the workplace, communication is critical, whether you're a manager, a leader, a salesperson, a negotiator or a trainer. Secondly, it helps people change how they think, behave and respond. So, for example, some techniques can help people who like a particular food not to like it. Or, like with my athletic clients who are nervous before an event or business clients before a presentation, there's a technique that could help you feel confident, calm, or relaxed, almost at the click of the fingers. NLP can also help people to get rid of phobias. And the third benefit is we can help people to replicate someone else's excellence. So, for example, if someone's brilliant at a particular skill that you want to be better at, you observe them and replicate their mindset and actions as much as possible.

NLP is extremely powerful, and like any powerful tool, sometimes it can be used manipulatively. Think about a computer – computers are useful but can be used to hack into other computers. It's never about the tool; it's only about the intention of the person using it. I've trained a lot of recruiters and non-recruiters, and if people are going to misuse NLP, I'll ask them to leave the course and never work with them.

So, one aspect of NLP is about influencing, and everyone wants to influence in the workplace. It's highly relevant for recruiters. There's a topic in NLP which helps us to understand why people respond in the way they do and helps us to influence them.

In NLP, this topic is called values. Values can be defined as 'what's important to someone'. Imagine you were looking to buy, for example, a pair of shoes. You would have in mind what's important to you or what you want from, or look for in, a pair of shoes (i.e. the Values'). An effective salesperson would ask you what you were looking for in a pair of shoes, ask a few more clarification questions, and then show you shoes that met your values. All things being equal, by knowing this information, the salesperson is more likely to sell than if they don't know this information. As an aside, many salespeople don't tend to do this; in my experience, they're too busy trying to talk and impress you rather than finding out what you actually want.

Here's a top tip for recruiters. Find out what prospective clients want from you, and demonstrate how you (and what you offer) will fit and meet their values. Then, you've got a much better chance of winning the business. How can you sell anything if you don't understand who you're selling to or what they really want? I've had experiences as a customer. I wanted a new car, so I went to a dealership. I was practically waving a chequebook. And the guy said, "Oh, we've got this, we've got that", and didn't ask what I wanted. I just walked out.

Results are really important to me – people getting what they want and achieving goals is paramount. I wish I had known this when I was 20, as, in my opinion, every young person would benefit from learning certain aspects of NLP.

Jeremy Lazarus – Key Takeaways

- The mindset for success is a positive attitude that anyone can develop, regardless of their background or circumstances.
- The mindset for success is based on five key beliefs:
  1) You can choose the life you want.
  2) You can achieve anything you desire with a compelling urge and a clear goal.
  3) You can learn any skill or attribute you need to succeed.
  4) You can overcome any obstacle or challenge you face.
  5) You can create value and make a positive difference in the world.
- The principles for success are six practical steps that help you apply the mindset for success:
  1) Know your purpose and passion.
  2) Set SMART goals and plan your actions.
  3) Take consistent and focused action.
  4) Seek feedback and learn from your mistakes.
  5) Surround yourself with positive and supportive people.
  6) Celebrate your achievements and enjoy the journey.
- Research and talk to people who have done what you want to do before starting a project or a venture. This can save you time, money and frustration.
- Surround yourself with mentors, coaches and peers who can support, guide, and challenge you in your journey. This can make the process more enjoyable and less risky.
- Learn from the best practices of successful people in any field. One example is NLP's six principles of success: know your goal, take action, gather information, be flexible,

operate from a physiology and psychology of excellence, and respect the present situation.
- Use a note-taking template to record information in your own words, absorb real-time information, and create action items for follow-up.

Contact Jeremy

www.thelazarus.com,
www.linkedin.com/in/jeremy-lazarus
jeremy@thelazarus.com
+44 (0)20 8349 2929

Jeremy's Q&A

What's your version of success?

Being free and able to be, do, and have whatever you truly want to be, do and have.

Top three books to read or listen to?

Conversations with God (Book 1). *Neale Donald Walsh.*
Think and Grow Rich. *Napoleon Hill.*
Mastering Leadership. *Anderson & Adams*

What's your favourite quote?

"Everything can be taken from a man but one thing: the last of the human freedoms—to choose one's attitude in any given set of circumstances, to choose one's own way." -Viktor Frankl, 'Man's Search for Meaning.'

"God grant me the serenity to accept the things I cannot change, the courage to change the things I can, and the wisdom to know the difference." Reinhold Niebuhr

What advice would you give your younger self?

Finances: Buy even more buy-to-let properties. Plan financially in more detail and even further ahead.

Business: Focus on building a large database from the very start. Pay attention to costs as well as revenues.

Relationships: Be more confident with women (in your teens and twenties); the worst that can happen is they say, 'No'.

Other: Leave home at 18 and go to university.

What is the best investment you have made, and why?

My first investment property. It set me on the path towards financial freedom and helped me realise that the benefits of renting properties outweigh the headaches.

My first personal development course; it set me on the path to the work I love doing.

What's your go-to productivity trick?

Make a list of tasks to be done today, with a timetable for the day.

If you could write a book about your life, what would the title be and why?

'My way'. Because that's how I've done it.

What's one thing you're learning now, and why is it important?

Leadership. I want to be an even better leadership coach and coach more leaders.

My mission is to (positively) touch the lives of millions of people, and working with leaders is probably the best and most accessible way for me to do that.

Who would you choose if you could trade places with anyone for a day?

No one. I am me. There are, however, lots of people I'd like to spend a day with, for example:

Sir Richard Branson (wealth and success strategies/mindset)
Roger Federer (sporting champion mindset)
Dalai Lama (spiritual learnings)

CHAPTER SIX

Jo Britton

(NLP)

About Jo

Jo is the founder of the award-winning business PACE Development. She is a certified and practising personal performance and leadership coach, working with entrepreneurs, leadership teams and professionals from various industry sectors, including the recruitment industry. She helps them find their edge, unlock the big stuff and optimise their performance without holding back or burnout. Before this, Jo held a range of executive leadership director and senior management positions in industry, including marketing and sales. She's an MBA and a BA(Hons) and is the UK's first and only certified neurosculpting® facilitator, which includes brain training, rewiring, performance, optimisation, flow and meditation all in one. She's an accredited coach with distinction, a certified DISC practitioner and a CMD-trained image consultant. Jo also judges for the UK business awards, is a visiting lecturer at Manchester Metropolitan University's Fashion Institute, a keynote speaker for Institute of Leadership and Management and a contributor to the Institute of Leadership and Management Edge publication. She's also the originator of the Mojo method and Mojo membership – a movement, community and membership for people who want to earn more, achieve more and believe in themselves.

In Jo's words:

My journey in sales and business development started in telesales cold calling. I learnt my craft there many years ago. I kept those skills because every time I went for a job, that's what people were interested in. In those days, cold calling included a phonebook, with which you would rip a page out of the directory and call Mr. or Mrs Smith and try and sell them replacement windows and doors. It was soul-destroying but also character-building. That was the start of thinking about unity and resilience, which took me into other sales and business development roles because I must have had resilience. My next role was business development in the manufacturing sector, with no product, no brand behind what we were selling, and no customer base. I had to knock on MD's doors in manufacturing and sell them this concept of developing their leaders. I knew nothing about manufacturing.

I was in my mid-20s, and although there was doubt because of all the rejection that sales bring, I built up a lot of resilience, and you need a resilient spirit in recruitment! In business development, you have incredible highs where it all comes together and feels fantastic. You think, "I can do this!" And then, the next minute, something falls through. It's a cliche, but it's a roller coaster. I progressed through the ranks in business development, and people on the outside would say that I was a high achiever. "She's got it all! She looks confident!" etc. But on the inside, there was always this self-doubt – a lack of confidence that affected me and held me back. That manifested in me feeling that I needed to prove myself all the time, so I'd work harder and harder and harder. Eventually, I held senior and director-level positions, but ultimately, it caught up with me. Let's say I burned myself out with high stress, worry and anxiety levels. "Am I good enough? Can I do this? I need to prove myself!"

I would go from city to city every day, get up at 4 am on a Monday, get the train from Manchester to London, and do a whole day there. Then I would come back the next day, go to Birmingham, and go to Gateshead the day after that. At the weekend, I'd be catching up with everything else. I thought I had to be superwoman, including everything at home. A lot of change was going on in the organisation I was working in, and I was on every change project; big transformational things and many things collided. I thought, "I'm not stressed," yet I'd be in and out of the GP with certain things, such as investigating my heart, rashes, and lesions. I would also have visual migraines. The doctor kept saying, "I think you are stressed!"

I didn't think I was stressed, to be honest, but it came out in my body physically. Because I wasn't feeling great, the doctor would say, "I think you are stressed; it's anxiety; take this medication". It didn't feel like there was another option. I would be on and off the medication, and the cycle would continue. Then, one day, I thought, "This corporate world is not for me anymore".

I'd always harboured an ambition to have my own business, but self-doubt always held me back. So finally, I decided to leave the corporate world and set up my own business PACE Development. The first year I had was amazing. I thought, "Hey, I can do this!" Then the pandemic hit. Overnight, all the corporate organisations I was working with withdrew contracts, and I absolutely spiralled with masses of anxiety and that whole self-doubt and lack of confidence again. Because we couldn't get an appointment with the GP at the start of the pandemic, I thought there had to be another way. There is no coincidence that I had panic attacks at this time.

To the outside world, I was a successful woman achieving all of this great stuff, so I decided to look deeper into the issue. I researched neuroscience; I used my coach tools. I put together my own little boot camp that was powerful and transformational. I'd lost my mojo, but after 14 days, I got my mojo back by doing a whole sequence of things. That's now become my 'mojo method', which I teach others. I believe we all have the capacity to achieve the big stuff we're made for without holding back and burning ourselves out. I built a framework on how to find our edge, and I work with people so we can do it optimally. And we get to have fun with it! It's all about getting clarity and focus and has transformational results with people.

Your mojo is your energy, enthusiasm, motivation and ability to harness it all when you're not feeling it or when there are obstacles and setbacks. Your mojo will help you to overcome challenges productively and healthily by taking inspired action.

The Mojo Framework

Steve: *Regarding mojo, I was talking with some mentees this week about those days when you wake up in the morning, walk into the office, and think, "I can't be bothered today. I can't be bothered to make any sales calls. Everyone's saying no to me anyway, clients aren't even in the offices, and they're not answering the phone."*

What would you suggest when you know you need to give yourself a kick yourself up the proverbial? How do you get started, find that motivation, and sustain it? What would you say to someone that just can't get motivated?

Jo: There are some great neurological tricks that you can use to your advantage. We have three neurotransmitters that are involved in motivation. When we harness our mojo, things happen, and it's magic. And we have these three neurotransmitters: dopamine, norepinephrine and acetylcholine. You might have heard of dopamine, which is like the reward chemical, and when we take a little bit of action, however small that is, it gives us the shot of dopamine. So, when you're not feeling it, take one little small action step. Imagine you're on a diet, and it's healthy food only, and you go to the supermarket to get all your healthy shopping.

Next to the supermarket is this amazing cake shop, and the smells coming out of the cake shop are fabulous, so you feel tempted, but dopamine tells you to walk past the cake shop. So, you walk past a cake shop because you'd rather make progress and go to the supermarket to get your healthy food. Norepinephrine is like the thing that says, 'Choose healthy food when you're in the supermarket!' Acetylcholine is the thing that stamps that experience into the brain so that you do it again the next time. So now we have all of these neurotransmitters dancing all the time. However, everybody's sweet spot is slightly different, so you will need to discover what your sweet spot is in terms of motivation and how to use it.

Regarding procrastination, there was a study done on teenage boys and girls who were given a task. They measured a mix of the three hormones for boys, who were high on dopamine, so they didn't perform very well in their task unless it was at the last minute. Then, only a deadline sparked their motivation, and then they performed very well. In contrast, it was the opposite for girls. Their adrenaline level was high, so when they were under pressure, they didn't perform as well, and their motivation dipped. It was better for the girls to put milestones in place and do tasks more slowly. So, this is how we're harnessing our chemistry around motivation to make it work for us. We have to play with how to trigger that dopamine and learn to use it for edge to perform at our best.

I thought I was a procrastinator, but now I'm at peace with that - I work well under pressure. I do my best work and motivate myself that way. You need to think about what sorts of things will motivate you. One of the reasons we don't take action or feel motivated is that things come up. Maybe something in the diary is going to get in the way, there's a change of something, someone walks into the office, and they're not in a particularly great mood, all of which are likely to affect our motivation;

the good news is that we can plan for obstacles. Equally, we have inner obstacles that we can plan for.

Sometimes we're not feeling motivated, so think, "What is it I'm going to do for that moment when I don't feel motivated? How do I overcome that hump in that lack of motivation?". You can plan for that. M and O in the Mojo method are Motivation and Overcoming Obstacles.

J in the mojo method is for joyful possibility. When our mojo is lacking, often it's because something's happened, there's a setback, and we flip quickly into negative thinking. People say to you, "Just think positively!" but that isn't helpful. As humans, we're not hardwired for positivity – positivity is a luxury. We are wired with a negativity bias, which is there to keep us safe. Therefore, we must work toward becoming positive. One way to move towards this is by thinking about what is possible now. "Is it possible that I can recover this deal? Is it possible that I can find a new deal? Yes, it's possible because I've done it before, and other people around me are doing it."

It's a mindset shift, and you will start feeling more positive. It will happen naturally. And the final one is that you must take action.

So, coming back to motivation, take a little action and ask yourself, "What is my intention in taking this action? Where is it on a scale of one to 10? How enthusiastic on a scale of one to 10 am I?" You might be 10 out of 10 in your intention but may feel seven out of 10 on your enthusiasm. So, ask yourself, "How would I make that a seven, an eight, a nine or a 10? What is it going to take to make me do that?"

When you combine all of these things, suddenly, you start harnessing your mojo, and you can keep moving forward in a much more productive way.

Trick the brain

Steve: *I love that – there's great value there. You've reminded me of a conversation we had a few weeks ago about when I began recruiting. Things used to go wrong, fees used to fall out, and people didn't turn up for the day they were due to start their new roles. I would quite often keep the details of the placement on my whiteboard in front of me, and it would sit there for days and weeks sometimes. I'd already mentally spent the commission on the fee that was going to allow me to hit my target. In turn, the negative emotion attached to the loss of that fee stayed with me every day. I would walk into work every morning, and the first thing I would see would be the whiteboard that reminded me that a fee didn't happen – it would stay with me and affect the way I worked, my motivation and my mojo every morning. Over time, I learnt that the quicker you remove that negativity, the better, so I had to come up with ways to snap myself out of it. I used to go outside, have a little scream or walk around the block, grab a posh coffee, then reset and start again. What do you do in these scenarios?*

Jo: When we hit a setback, I have two characters that I refer to because it helps explain some of the brain stuff in layman's terms. I'm not a neuroscientist, so if anybody is reading this, I apologise, but it's how I understand, apply it, and allow myself to help others.

If you're stressed about a lost opportunity or a failed deal in the office, and you're in a moment where you decide to go for a walk to clear your head, you are helping to calm the limbic centre in the brain, which is the fear centre, the stress centre; the part that in the brain keeps us safe and alive. It's part of the brain that is constantly looking for threats. If it sees a real threat, like a car hurtling towards us, or an imagined one, such as "Where am I going to get my next deal from? I'm falling!!" It reacts the same way – sending all the stress chemicals around the body, preparing us to mobilise, or in other words, "GET OUT OF THE WAY!" fight or flight. You might know the limbic centre as the fight-flight centre, and I refer to this part of the brain as Frankenstein. In those moments where we've had a setback like the perceived failure, it doesn't make us feel good. It activates that fight-flight centre and makes us feel like we're under threat. I always say that Frankenstein is not the brightest of people, but he is a life-saving gift when we need him, such as when the car is hurtling toward us.

We need to mobilise to get out of the way, and he gives us the 'go juice' sending vital resources around the body that will help to save our life; our muscles contract, our breathing shallows, our heart rate quickens and our digestion goes offline – ready to fight or flee. However, in the working world, whether you're in business development or recruitment, those threats aren't real threats to life; they're perceived and imagined, yet they still activate Frankenstein in the same way. So, we need to learn to calm him. Taking a walk and deep breaths are really good ways to calm those fight-flight circuits. When you do that, you can flip to what I call 'Einstein', our prefrontal cortex. It's where we access our best human qualities that we need to perform well. Think of all the best qualities you would include on a CV – 'I'm rational', 'I'm motivated', 'I achieve goals', 'I'm creative', 'I'm a problem solver' – that's your prefrontal cortex,

There's an inverse relationship between Frankenstein and Einstein. It's like a seesaw in the brain. If Frankenstein's at the top of the seesaw, using all those stress, hormones and chemicals, Einstein is at the bottom and has gone to sleep. We can't be in both Einstein and Frankenstein at the same time.

This is our neuro chemistry at work – when we calm our Frankenstein part of the brain, guess what happens? We bring Einstein back online and access our best qualities that help us move forward. If you think about it that way, it can really help. Once you've been for a walk, taken some deep breaths and calmed down, it's likely you will feel a lot better, and you could find ways to problem solve, get creative, get back on the phone and move forward more positively. Of course, this is a practice, and it doesn't come easy, especially at the start. It's about continual effort.

How to not give up

Procrastination isn't laziness. About 90% of the time, it's connected to some kind of fear we have. Fear of rejection is a big one for many people, as is fear of success, failure, succeeding and then failing, fear of feeling embarrassed, ashamed, humiliated, judged, and fear of change. These emotions are wired subconsciously as neuro patterns that become our 'go-to' scripts that we access automatically without realising it. They are wired hard and fast, usually as a result of an experience that we have had in a highly charged emotional state. The brain is a prediction machine. I don't mean the crystal ball gazing kind of stuff. Instead, the brain works on prediction scripts to navigate the world. We've got the prediction script to get up in the morning, walk, brush our hair and clean our teeth etc. We also have scripts in the form of beliefs or stories we may tell ourselves, either consciously or subconsciously, which influence our behaviour, actions and results. Some of these scripts propel us forward, and some hold us back.

Suppose we've had a highly charged, unpleasant emotional experience where we've been rejected. At that moment, our brain is neuroplastic – neuroplasticity is the term science gives us for the way we learn things. We wire a fear-based script designed to keep us safe in case that situation occurs. We then access and retrieve it when we perceive we need it. Some of us have wired a fear of rejection through an uncomfortable experience. So, in procrastination, the first thing to be aware of is which story is playing out. "What is it that? Why is it that I am not taking action here? What is it I'm afraid of?" These are great questions to help us notice. Then we can do some inner work around it because usually, the brain is working automatically without realising it, which is the limbic Frankenstein brain in action. It's fast and automatic, and at the moment, it'll pull that fear-based script from our memory bank. That's where we tend to default because it's safe, predictable, and hardwired. Maybe this plays out for you like the 'what if game?' "Well, what if I do this and it goes wrong? What if I fail when I make that next call? What if I'm wrong?" and this can make us feel bad. If we access that memory again, we resurface that body reaction and those neurochemicals that went with that experience again, and we add layers of what I call 'dirt' to it, so it becomes stronger. The more we use that pattern, the stronger it gets and becomes more automatic.

So, how do we flip the switch? First is to become aware that the switch has descended into a downward spiral. So, instead of asking, "What if I'm rejected?" flip it and ask ourselves a better question, like "What if I succeed on the next call? What if this next call opens up a massive opportunity with this client who says how brilliant I am, who refers me to more people, helps me find more clients, more candidates!"

Flipping is a fast and effective way to tap into your mojo, but like any other technique, it will take practise before it becomes a pattern of habit. The more you practice, the more it will become your default setting. If you're feeling rejected or not feeling great, become aware of it, flip it, and practice, practice, practice. That's when you start optimising your performance, and that's when you can enjoy life as you do it, start seeing results that you've never seen before, and start taking action as you've never done before.

Dealing with pressure

Steve: *The key takeaway is self-awareness. Understanding that you're having negative thoughts, and they are preventing you from taking that next step.*

The last time we chatted, we had an honest discussion about my entrepreneurial journey and that I'd really pushed the boat out the last couple of years. I was honest with you and told you that I ended up in hospital in October last year, which was quite scary. I'm still on medication now for high blood pressure and various other things. I wouldn't call it a revelation, but in terms of being honest with myself; about how I was working and feeling. I was trying to do everything I could and doing too much. Showing my vulnerability isn't something I'm used to doing, but in this instance, I had to hold a white flag temporarily.

Is a situation like mine common with your mentees and the people that you coach? How do you go about dealing with it?

Jo: I don't think we talk about the real pressures of life enough, and therefore, we think we're the only ones feeling those emotions, and therefore something is wrong with us. We run our bodies in this stressful state for long periods that are not sustainable. The Frankenstein brain, with its chemicals and hormones flooding the body at an elevated level over a prolonged period, is setting our body up for bad health, like heart issues, diabetes etc. This was happening to me, but I was ignoring it and running my body in an unsustainable state. Recognising it is so important. Mind and body are on both sides of the same coin, neurologically and neurophysiologically. We can't separate them because what you think affects the body's response, and what you're feeling in your body can affect how and what you think. So, if you are accessing negative thought patterns, you're repeatedly sending stress hormones around your body, and then you will feel it in your body. And when it doesn't feel good in the body, you may start worrying even more. For some of us, it may be sweaty palms, tense muscles, headaches, or it may be the heart. For me, it was a racing heart, palpitations and tightness in the chest, and we're not supposed to run the body like that for long periods. Suppose an animal in the wild is under threat; you will notice that once that threat has passed, it will shake its body, which dissipates the stress. Yet, humans aren't taught the tools to regulate the body. Giving your body a vigorous 60-second shake can really help you too! It's super important to recognise how the mind and body are working together and try to press the pause button when you can. That is the best thing to do.

It irritates me to see too many of the 5 am entrepreneurs who say, "I work 20 hours a day; I don't need to sleep!"

No – sleep is the *most* important thing. Everything starts with sleep. All of this macho stuff that goes on in business is essentially fooling ourselves, as you will burn yourself out. And then, when it gets to that point, it's a life-changing moment. It's important to know that you've arrived at that point and reach out to people. Sometimes we feel like we don't have somebody to talk to without blame, shame or judgment because we're always blaming, shaming and judging ourselves. If you're an entrepreneur or in sales, it can be lonely and can feel like you're carrying the weight of the world on your shoulders. People often don't want to burden others with their feelings. So, a big part of my role as a coach and confidante is listening and helping challenge people's thinking in a supportive way, without blame, shame or judgment. However, it is up to you if you want to do something about it.

Find Positive People

We all have the capacity to be absolutely amazing if we learn how to harness our strengths, talents and skills. A lot of the time, we don't even realise that we have them. Having somebody to walk by your side and raise awareness about your strengths will help considerably. Some organisations can be quite toxic, which will have a massive draining effect on how you feel in body and mind. So, another tip is to surround yourself with optimistic people who will challenge and support you helpfully and productively. People who will lift and support you, who you can collaborate, connect and communicate with. We're social beings, and we should always remember to reach out.

Steve: *It's so true. One of the best journeys I've had over the last nine years is investing in my education, paying to go to seminars and having coaches in various guises and forms. I wouldn't be where I am now without having the right people around me. From your perspective, who are the biggest influences? Who are the people around you that have changed your perception, career, journey or life?*

Jo: I have a coach and a mentor; they are two different things for me. My mentor is 26 years old. He's an entrepreneur, scaling his business at a super quick speed, and he's doing it the way I want to – he's further ahead of me. If you want to check him out, he is Chris Taylor on Instagram. The reason he's my mentor is that when I was not in a good place, I wanted to find people with different perspectives and optimism, and he was smashing it. So, he became my mentor, and it has been amazing. Your mentor can be any age.

For me, a coach helps you move from where you are now to where you want to be without giving you the answers, but it can get the best out of you. They can challenge, support, and raise awareness in you so that you take inspired action and always come up with solutions. I have many coaches in my life that are on and offline and from books etc. However, the other influential person in my life is Lisa Wimberger, who started my journey with neurosculpting®. Lisa is the founder and creator of neurosculpting®. I read her book, 'New Beliefs New Brain,' and learnt how everything is wired and what we can do about it. I learnt neurosculpting® as a practice to harness the neuroplasticity in your brain and rescript the stories and beliefs that hold you back or create ones that will propel you forward using a unique five-step process. Lisa's life was under threat through seizures that she had had due to being struck by lightning when she was 15. But unfortunately, the traditional medical profession said, "There's nothing we can do!"

The seizures got so bad that her body was playing dead at one point. So, she developed this amazing transforming practice, which is what I'm practising now. I'm lucky to have her as a coach; Lisa has greatly influenced me. She's trained me to become the first certified practitioner in the UK.

There were other mentors I didn't realise at the time were mentors, but they looked out for me and gave me advice. Another influence is my grandmother. She was a refugee at the end of World War Two in the UK and, at 14, had been taken away to Germany by the Nazis and never returned home. She had nothing when she arrived in the UK; she had to learn to speak English and work hard. When I think back on all of the qualities and things I value, they have come from her; hard work, determination, and being generous with people, whether that's time or money. Also, in love and affection, she was a real influence in my life. Only recently have I begun to discover where we take our values from.

Knowing what matters most to us is important because it makes us have more positive life experiences, which means we perform better.

Jo Britton's Advice in Summary

- Start small and build resilience through practice.
- Learn from every rejection and keep your skills sharp.
- Believe in your potential; don't let self-doubt hold you back.
- Focus on the positive aspects of your job and celebrate the small wins.
- Take care of your physical and mental health to avoid burnout.
- Recognise the signs of stress and anxiety in your body and seek help.
- Consider starting your own business if you feel limited in the corporate world.
- Research neuroscience and use coaching tools to overcome self-doubt and find your edge.
- Create your own mojo method to maintain energy, enthusiasm, and motivation.
- Use the Mojo Framework to find clarity, focus, and inspiration to achieve your goals.
- Practice taking inspired action even when you don't feel motivated.
- Surround yourself with supportive and encouraging people who believe in you.

Dealing with Procrastination:

- Procrastination is often about doubt and fear, not laziness.
- Fear of rejection, success, failure, embarrassment, judgment, and change can all contribute to procrastination.

- Our brain creates prediction scripts that become automatic, and some of these hold us back.
- To overcome procrastination, become aware of the story you're telling yourself and do some inner work around it.
- Instead of asking negative questions, flip the script and ask yourself better questions to harness your mojo and practice this new pattern.

Dealing with Pressure:

- Self-awareness is key to understanding how negative thoughts affect you and prevent you from taking the next step. It's important to recognise the real pressures of life and not run our bodies in a stressful, unsustainable state.
- Mind and body are connected, and negative thought patterns can send stress hormones around the body, leading to physical symptoms.
- Recognising and addressing pressure is crucial for maintaining good health.

How to contact Jo.

There are two places I usually hang out; on Instagram, follow me at jobritton.mojo and on LinkedIn, look for Jo Britton. I'm always here to reach out if you have a question, and I'm all about giving as much value as possible. There is no pressure, no charge – just reach out and have a conversation. Take the first step. I think that's always the important thing. If you're struggling with something, don't sit there feeling all alone. Take the first step and reach out.

LinkedIn	https://uk.linkedin.com/in/jobrittonpace
Instagram	@jobritton.mojo
Email	jo@pacedevelopment.co.uk

Jo's Q&A

What's your version of success?

To go to bed each night feeling fulfilled that I've given my best and helped others give their best, too, so they can live a longer, happier, healthier and wealthier life.

Top three books to read or listen to?

'New Beliefs, New Brain' by Lisa Wimberger
'High Performance: Lessons from the Best on Becoming Your Best' by Jake Humphrey and Prof Damian Hughes
'Dare to Lead' by Brene Brown

What's your favourite quote?

'If you're interested, you'll do what's convenient. If you're committed, you'll do whatever it takes.' John Assaraf

What advice would you give your younger self?

Believe in yourself – do your inner work so that nothing holds you back. Get yourself a mentor and surround yourself with people who will inspire you. Worry less about failure and what others think of you. Failing is an inevitable part of success. It's simply feedback and learning, so take it as such. Use it productively as fuel to help you keep moving forward.

What is the best investment you have made, and why?

In a mentor and a coach. Both play different roles in my life and are worth their weight in gold. My mentor is a few steps ahead of where I want to get to. He offers me advice, guidance, and accountability and helps me to execute my plans. My coach is different. She helps me to find solutions for myself when I'm stuck by challenging my thinking and raising awareness when I'm getting in my own way because she's skilled at asking purposeful questions and listening to understand rather than reply.

What's your go-to productivity trick?

For me, there are many reasons why we're not as productive as we could be. This could include:

- Lack of clarity or organisation around what we're doing.
- Distractions (inner ones such as unhelpful thoughts we're having as well as outer ones like the usual email and social media notifications going off, unexpected events occurring).
- Tiredness.
- Overwhelm (too much on your list/not enough hours in the day).
- Trouble getting/staying motivated.
- Procrastination.
- Unhelpful daily habits, routines and rituals.

I don't just have one productivity trick; I use a combination.

Firstly, I became aware of what was causing my lack of productivity. Is it because I'm unclear about what I'm trying to achieve or the desired result? If so, I write this out and put a plan around it to organise myself.

Is it because I'm not feeling motivated? If so, I'll take some action and then a bit more to build momentum and get a shot of dopamine – the reward chemical in the brain to feel motivated.

Is it because I'm having unhelpful thoughts – like "What if I don't succeed?" Then, I become aware of my thoughts and flip them to something more helpful, like "What if I do succeed?"

If I'm procrastinating, I'll ask myself what I'm afraid of and work on releasing that. Procrastination is usually always the result of some kind of fear we have. To tackle that, you'll find you make better progress.

"Are my habits, routines and rituals aligned with what I want to get done?" If not, I'll look at what I need to stop/start doing as daily habits. I'm a big fan of habit stacking – i.e. building on an existing habit to create a new one. Habits are just neural patterns, and your brain doesn't know the difference between good and bad habits. My job is to shift as many habits to ones that will serve me to be most productive.

If you could write a book about your life, what would the title be and why?

'How to knock out Nina Nitpicker and find your mojo to believe and achieve.'

It would be a how-to/self-help book for people living life through a fear-based, anxiety or self-doubt-based lens. That was always me from a young age – not feeling good enough, confident enough and having my Nina Nitpicker imposter holding me back and draining my mojo. It would be concerned with why this happens and how this happens. And what you can do about it. I work with many capable people who deserve a better life for themselves, but their subconscious patterns, stories and beliefs can hijack and inhibit them. I would write about how, and when you know what's going on, you can make change happen with some relatively simple techniques that we're not taught about from a young age and make a massive difference.

What's one thing you're learning now, and why is it important?

I'm obsessed with learning about how our brain and nervous systems work, so I'm always researching and learning more about neuroscience, particularly neuroplasticity discoveries. At its most basic, neuroplasticity is the term science gives us for how we learn. I love to explore how the brain wires up and how its neural connections change over time due to our environment, thinking, behaviour and emotions. While it was once thought that an adult brain had become hardwired after adolescence, thanks to technological developments such as functional MRI scanning, scientists have discovered brain plasticity happens throughout our life. What does this mean, and why is it important? Our brain is much more flexible than we thought. So, it debunks the 'old dog/new tricks' myth. We don't have to believe how we are is how we must stay. This has exciting potential to help us overcome fear-based thinking, which may sabotage or hold us back from achieving our goals and aspirations. Science is starting to prove that we can change how we think by modifying our thought patterns.

And I support my clients to do this by using a powerful brain entrainment process called Neurosculpting®, which helps people to release patterns of anxiety, stress and fear and helps them to build confidence and self-belief. This ultimately means they can optimise their performance without burning out and achieve results at an accelerated pace.

Who would you choose if you could trade places with anyone for a day?

I've been thinking about this question for days and have struggled with it. And I've realised it's because I now love being me and my life and how I'm experiencing it. I don't want to change places, even for a day with anyone. It might sound like a cop-out, but it's not. It's just made me realise that all the work I'm constantly doing on myself to improve myself and live a more fulfilled, happier life has been paying off. And that's really profound for me!

CHAPTER SEVEN

Lee Eldridge

(High Performance)

About Lee

L ee's life passion is coaching people to achieve their full leadership potential. He enables clients to take back control, create time for themselves, develop their ability to be focused, and help individuals achieve their goals. Throughout his 20-year career, he has worked with athletes and business executives in elite environments, including professional rugby and football players, world-ranked tennis players and C-suite executives at multinational companies. He holds an MSc in human performance and a BSc in sport science and coaching. He is the founder and performance director of 'Cognitive Athlete', a bespoke human performance coaching company on a mission to lead elite business executives towards obtaining and sustaining optimal results over the long term.

Lee's own words:

Steve: *I want to find and separate what makes an average and elite performer. What would you say are some of the characteristics that separate the two?*

Lee: I think that it's important to understand that consistency plays a huge role in everything that we do. And from my point of view, I've seen that high performers do things consistently well. It's not to say that average performers don't, but high performers understand what they have to work on. Everybody can work hard at exercise or business, but true high performers know what they need to focus on, which helps shift that needle. Especially when you get to an elite level, you won't make huge jumps in increasing your performance or being more productive. It's about trying to get a little bit better each day, or each session or however that might look. And if we think from a professional sporting role, you take the top football players, all they've done throughout their career is just got that little bit better year on year. Hence, you or I could never become as fit as a professional football player because we've left it for too long. But from a business point of view, you have to understand that there's a slight difference between professional sports and elite business. Obviously, in professional sports, we're talking about maximising that player's potential and that player's career for a short period of time. But with business, we're looking at more of an endurance event. Suppose you want to become a CEO or a leader of a country. Committing to the long game, developing knowledge, education, and relationships, will enable you to gain the experience needed to understand and pursue your desired position. So, if you think of it as an endurance event, then we're talking more about how to optimise your day-to-day, week-to-week, and month-to-month. And in a nutshell, the best high performers are what I call 'proactive reactives'. What I mean by that is everybody is an agile leader or has an agile company. Even before COVID, it was a mark of how good you are as a company to be able to pivot and change. The difficulty stems from the fact that agility, like in sport, requires one to decelerate, alter course, and then re-accelerate, all of which take effort. There's no difference in business. Yet, what we haven't done is we haven't really sat back and thought, 'How much energy is this taking out of us, and how much are we demanding of the people around us?' To be proactive and prepared for agile situations, consistently activate core skills for personal and professional development within your company. This positions you to effectively respond and adapt when reactive moments arise. Whereas if you're constantly reactive, you're always coming from a place of stress or low energy and less able to pivot and move into the next area.

Gaining back control

Steve: *I think COVID meant that people had to react differently, more quickly, and pivot or divert their attention, and thus productivity went out the window because survival became paramount. So, if you're in a position where you lack control over your days and weeks, how do you grab that control back? How'd you get to the point where you draw the line and say, "Today is going to be different?"*

Lee: I think the first step is to create some awareness. It's interesting to talk to people who don't realise they lack control to a certain degree. They wake up, grind away, hustle, whatever you want to call it; the day finishes, they go to bed, and it's Groundhog Day. So, the first step is to think, "What's going on here?"

The second thing is to think about who controls you. A lot of the CEOs or C-suite people I work with have limited control of their diaries. It's their PAs or EAs that are the filters. If I am working with a client, if they've got a very good PA or EA, life becomes much easier for me because you're trying to get to see that person. So that's kind of the key stakeholder with some of these individuals. And then it's to have a discussion along the lines of, "Where can I carve out some time during the day that's mine, that I control, and I don't allow anybody to book a meeting with me. When can I get an opportunity to do my most important tasks?"

At the moment, I'm seeing people on back-to-back Zoom meetings, and then they do their work late afternoon or late evening, in some cases. I think from a performance point of view, especially a cognitive point of view, it's not ideal to be able to do your most important work when you're fatigued at the end of the day. So, what we should do instead is carve out some time during the day instead. For most people, it's between 9-11 am when they can get their most important tasks done and focus on what they're trying to do. The problem is that it is the main time that most people have meetings. So, carve out some time during the day, which can start out as little as 15 – 30 minutes. I found that working with these individuals is that once they get half an hour in the block, it's quite easy to stretch out to 40 minutes or an hour. They begin to understand how long they can concentrate. For most people, 100% concentration only lasts for around 90 minutes and then our performance drops, and we lose concentration.

The statistics say that, on average, people get interrupted from work every six minutes, and the truth is, we can't multitask. People think they can, but we can't – all that we do is task switch. We go from one thing to the next to the next, especially when we're looking at high-cognitive tasks. Plus, there's a gap between each of the switches, and thus it takes us energy and time to catch up. That's why if we think about it from a Zoom meeting point of view, most people are a couple of minutes late. They've got off a call, they've jumped straight on the next call, and their brain is trying to process what just happened but also get up to speed with what is happening in the present and what will be discussed. So that brief two to five minutes is heavily demanding on our brains, and it doesn't need to be if we were able to finish that meeting five minutes earlier, make some notes about what's just happened, and read through the agenda of what's coming up. By doing that, they're on the first steps to taking back some control. Of course, what you do in that time is down to you. If you do need to do some physical activity, for example, prioritise that.

Imagine that you might have anywhere between 10 to 20 calls a day; it means that 20 times a day, those little five-minute blocks amount to a huge cognitive load. So, task blocking or time blocking is the way to go. Try to put all of your tasks together – if you're answering emails, dedicate half an hour to answering emails because you get into the flow as opposed to jumping forward and back. Now, don't get me wrong, there are some roles, such as an assistant, where you need to check emails and push stuff forward. But still, those individuals need to take time during the day to work on their most important tasks – the things that are going to help them improve or help their processes improve. That's what it is at the end of the day – it's not how hard you work; it's how good your processes are. As soon as your processes are good, then you can put hard work into that process; the more hard work you put into the process, the better the outcome. Whereas if your process is not great and you just keep plugging away, it's not going to lead anywhere.

Work/Life Balance

Steve: *I'm a firm believer that process makes you more efficient. I mentioned in my book 'Top Biller' about the ability to have what I called 'the extended time people'. It's not the fact that some people have more time than others; it's that if things are planned properly and coordinated, you can maximise what you're doing in any given task, at any point, and get more done. Some people say, "It's okay for Steve; he's got more time than the rest of us." Well, it's not true – I haven't got more time than anybody else. I am simply rigid about how I approach each day. I knew the output before I started my day. I know a lot of people don't work that way, certainly in sales. I often talk about recruiters being very flamboyant, salesy, out there, loving the people connection, and going out and meeting people. They are very good at outward sales, but quite often, they'll leave a trail of destruction behind them in terms of process. Some of them are highly successful people, but they often don't know how they've got there because it's just been a blaze of glory along the journey. I'm probably the extreme opposite* *of that; I know exactly what I'm doing at any point during the day. I still succeed, but I use a different method. One of the things I often struggle with, and the thing my wife constantly reminds me of, is that we have two beautiful young boys. I struggle to balance work and life to make sure that I don't spend every hour of every day working to ensure the future is secure, yet forgetting I've got to take the kids to the park and play football with them. How do you balance the feeling of guilt when you're perhaps in the office and you should be somewhere else?*

Lee: I think there's no such thing as work/life balance; I think there's just life. And work is a pillar of your life. And once people understand that, or you start to think about it, you can see that there are multiple pillars in everyone's life. So, you might be a manager, but you also might be a husband and wife, father, mother, sports person, an amateur sports person, and they're all pillars in your life. And if we put all our time into one pillar, and something goes wrong in that pillar, and we look for the others to support us, they're not there. I've seen it happen with CEOs that are spending anywhere between 80 and 100 hours, plus travel at work, lose their job, and have a poor relationship with their partner, they don't understand what's going on within their kid's lives, and they're unhealthy because they haven't given any time to that.

You must make sure that you are spending time in each of your pillars and understand that by spending time in those areas, you're actually improving all the other areas. So, if Steve, for example, has a happy marriage, and a good relationship with his children, there's no doubt in my mind that he'll be more productive at work. There'll be less worry, there'll be less thinking about what's going on, and you'll be able to engage 100% in that one thing. We are really bad at not being engaged in our tasks. You can be sitting there having dinner with your family, and you're probably thinking, "Oh, I need to do such and such tomorrow", and as a result, you're not actually with them in that room. You must make sure that you carve out the time to be engaged in that one activity you are doing at the time. This is the main reason I think that a lot of the individuals I work with are into their endurance events. It's madness; I don't know why, if you're a CEO, and you work 70 hours a week, you want to go and train for a triathlon. But what that does, is it puts you in the middle of nowhere, not on your phone, and all you can do is focus on running on that road, or cycling, or swimming, or whatever it is. It's a moment of engagement in that.

Now let's bring that back to not being truly engaged at work. By that, I mean that things are coming in, you're being very reactive, and you're not dedicating that engagement time to the thing that you should be engaging. How often, when you're in a Zoom meeting, can you see the person scrolling through their emails or talking to somebody on their phone? They're not engaged in the conversation. I've been in workshops and delivered workshops whereby people are on their phones or looking at emails, and I say, "Either be really engaged in this workshop or don't and leave!" It's tough, to be honest with people, but it's important.

Also, when people say that "they are too busy", it's not true. Instead, they mean, "You're not one of my priorities." We're always prioritising, so being too busy is a nice way of saying, "You're not one of my priorities". I'd much prefer people to be completely honest and say, "Hey, look, you're not on my list of most important things, or you're not on my list of people I need to speak to today."

That's how simple it is; you're not too busy to go out and exercise – exercise is not one of your priorities. If exercise was one of the things that you wanted to do or needed to do, you would make time for it. And we only make time for things when we put them in our diary, as it's much easier to move something around when it's in the diary, as opposed to trying and make time out of fresh air.

Practising full engagement

Steve: *I'm a firm believer that if I'm in a meeting, my phone is on silent. If I am talking to someone in the office, and it's an important conversation, I shift away from my laptop. That way, you can be engaged in that very moment. I'm not perfect by any stretch, and quite often, I can have conversations whilst scrolling or reading an email. I have to be self-aware to say, "I'm really sorry; can you say that again? I wasn't listening." Or "I was preoccupied and/or distracted." We used to have management and director meetings that had a box at the front of the meeting room. You had to put your phones in the box before entering the meeting room so that everyone could be fully engaged. Are there any tips other than turning your phone off? What can we practice on a daily basis?*

Lee: Look at what tasks you're going to do in a time period. If you don't have goals, or you don't have things to get done, you won't do them; you'll shift and start to preoccupy your brain with something else. Make sure that you set clear goals, and at the end of that time period, you give yourself some feedback, "was I focused or was I not? Why not? What were the reasons?"

Set up an environment where you can concentrate. Most people (depending on where they are working) now have noise-cancelling headphones, especially if you have young children, and they're running around the house, or you're in the office. You must make sure that when you're in the flow state, you stay there as it helps with peak performance; it helps us think differently; you don't want any disruptions because as soon as you're disturbed or disrupted, you're out of that state. And then you need to get back into it. Flow states are well-researched and well-documented to improve performance. McKinsey did a study on it by getting people into that state, and it was a 500% improvement in productivity. It's the main reason why extreme athletes do what they do or why people get addicted to certain activities because it gives you this feeling of timelessness, effortlessness and richness. You know when you're in that moment, when you've put that hour in your day, and you get into it, and it's gone in a flash. The alarm goes off, and "Wow, that was an hour, and I got a large chunk of my work done!"

They are some of the things that you can build in. If you are in an office situation, try to get away from people. I know it seems weird, but there should be times during the course of the day when you can find a quiet place in the office. Some offices now have pods that you can go into, or you can use a spare meeting room. Get in there, know what you need to do in the hour, and just start working away on it.

How to deal with knockbacks and rejection

James Clear, who wrote Atomic Habits, talks about this, and this is a double-edged sword of goal setting. James says if we think about two football teams playing, they both have exactly the same ambition to win the game, but one team wins. And it's not because the other team didn't have the right ambition, it's just that the other team had better processes in place. What we need to understand is that goals and targets are there for benchmarking and they're identifying how we are doing. Because if you don't make your goal, you get demotivated. If you hit your goal, you're really happy. If you succeed, you think, "Wow, I could have done more, maybe!" And that's the human brain- that's the reason why people who climbed Mount Everest get all the way down to the bottom, and their mojo is gone. They think, "Well, what do I do next?"

The climber that reached 14 peaks in seven months, I bet he's now thinking, "Okay, what challenge next? What can I do now? How can I top it?"

I think that once you create a bit of a plan, or an understanding around where or who you want to become, it doesn't really matter if you hit those goals or not. If you hit those goals, you need to learn why you hit them; if you didn't hit the goals, you need to know why you didn't hit them. Having an understanding that in life, we control very little. Even people who are very healthy can get struck down with a sickness. So, think about what you can influence. Obviously, in recruitment, if a guy doesn't turn up to work on a Monday, you don't have any control over that. People beat themselves up about things that they have no control over all the time. "I couldn't get to work because my car broke down," and they're all stressed and panicky – but it's not their fault. They could have influenced it by making sure the car was serviced etc., but I think that people are very hard on themselves these days.

People think, "I want to be a high performer, I need to be disciplined, and I need to work hard". Yeah, you do, but you also need to understand that things are not always going to go your way. Take the emotion out of the situation, become more disassociated with what's going on, and use it as a learning experience. I'm working my way through Jimmy Carr's new book, and it's interesting how he talks about being a comedian and that you've got to get used to failure because it's going to happen. I imagine it's probably one of the worst things when you make a joke and no one laughs – you get immediate feedback. It's a failure, and you've got nowhere to hide. I think that people use 'not hitting goals as "Oh, that's it – out the window." "I haven't lost this weight – the training program was rubbish." "My diet was rubbish!"

That's all quite over the top. I think, "Right, how can I learn from this?"

I'm not sure if it was Sir Alex Ferguson or Sir Clive Woodward who said, "We learn more about a team when we win than when we fail, but we still have to learn."

On feedback

We all talk about the skill of giving feedback, and yet nobody often touches on the skill of receiving feedback. It's a mindset thing to a certain degree so that anything that person can say or do is down to you and how you interpret it. Everyone says that you need to be positive, and to a certain degree it's true, but sometimes, especially in high-performance sports, the truth needs to come out. Honesty needs to be there for the relationship to develop. I can remember when a mentor of mine and I had a really honest discussion. He used an analogy I liked. He said, "I'm a pilot, I'm the captain of the plane, and you're the co-pilot. If you don't tell me that there's a mountain over there, we're both going to crash, and we're both not going to be here. So, you need to start working with me and realise that I want you, someday, to be able to fly a plane."

That got me thinking about moments previously whereby people have given me bad feedback, and my immediate reaction was emotional, and I would think that they didn't like me. If I think back now, that feedback was probably some of the most motivating moments I went through at those times. I think it's an important skill, as a high performer, that you must develop and understand. There is a lack of feedback in business. In sports, it's huge; if you think about it, as you increase the level of performance in sports, you get better and more frequent coaching, you get access to stats, GPS, running, and speed touches etc. Yet, as you move through the layers of business, when you become a CEO, or you become the top person of a company, it's hard to get honest feedback from the people around you because everyone wants to play a game. Nobody wants to tell the boss honestly what's happening because when a promotion or bonus time comes around, people think, "Well, my honesty might affect the boss's decision!" Once you get to that top stage, you need to find people who give you honest feedback.

On Stress

The term stress has negative connotations – we hear it all the time people are 'too stressed,' or 'I've got so much on I feel really stressed'. But stress is what's got that individual to that point. If you want to get bigger muscles or be stronger and fitter, you need to stress the body and stress the muscles, so the body says, "I didn't like that; I'm going to come back a little bit stronger!"

And that is what life's about. The problem comes when there's too much stress or things happen too quickly, and we can't cope with it, and we panic, and we can't break it down in our head to deliver those small bouts of stress. That also comes about with no sleep, diet, nutrition, movement, all those things that we all know we should look after from a health and wellbeing point of view, but they get pushed to one side.

In fitness, it's important to set goals, not just going for a run or whatever – you need to be a bit more specific about it. If you want to run the London Marathon, for example, you know you have to run 26 miles, and you can reverse engineer what you need to be doing. Know how far you can run in 30 minutes, and what your heart rate is. All these data points help.

I see so many people go to the gym, and they walk in, and they just start looking around for the first machine. "What am I gonna do? Oh, look, somebody is using the bench press? Well, I can't do that."

I suggest you go into the gym with a piece of paper, or something written on your phone with your intentions for your workout. You must agree you will do exactly what it says on your phone or the paper. At the end of the session, you can ask yourself, "Did I do it? No. Okay, why not? What do I need to change?" By doing that, you're giving feedback to your brain, and it lets you begin to see the improvements.

If we put it from a business point of view, and I turn around to the CEO, and I say, "What was your profit and loss last year and your revenue per person?" I bet they could come up with that data at any time. They simply don't use that understanding in every part of their life. It just takes a little bit of time and a little bit of crafting.

Many people run a marathon and then stop running. Yet, they should use the marathon as a goal to become somebody or an outcome. And the outcome is to be a runner. And that's what it's all about. There's no point going to the gym for five hours one day in a week – you need to go five times – you need to show up and keep that momentum going. I think that breeds success, and it's tough.

Nobody interviews CEOs that failed, even though lots of CEOs do fail. I think that we would learn more from their failures than from the top people that succeed.

One piece of advice

Steve: *If there's one single piece of advice that you would offer, what would that be?*

Lee: The first step is to have some awareness of what is going on. As a salesperson, I'm sure you know exactly what your numbers were last week or the week before. But you should also ask yourself, where am I? Be honest with yourself from a 360 point of view. "What is my health like? What is my sleep like? What's my work like? How are all of my relationships? To build up a picture of moving forward for the next year, where would I need to be? If I was in those better places, what would it look like? What would it feel like?"

Start that process – it can be tough and demoralising if things are a struggle, but for me, it is the first step. When I work with clients, I want to work with the right people. The kind of people that want to work. So, we need to get to the stage where the client can say "I've realised that I'm currently working in a way that's non-sustainable, and there's going to be bigger problems down the line." So many people I speak to say, "I feel like I'm just surviving at the moment. I just can't wait till Christmas." And I say, "Yeah, but what happens in January?"

"Well, you know, January's a new year with new goals. We've got to push ourselves in the new year". They say.

But it's not sustainable. Everyone talks about sustainable energy, in what we're trying to do for global warming, but nobody talks about sustainable energy in people. I think once you create that awareness, it gives you a bit of a blueprint to help you get through things.

If you have friends that are abrupt and honest, get their feedback. Don't go to the nice guy, because the nice guy will say "you're doing well". Instead, you need to hear the negative and then not have an emotional reaction. Realise that it comes from a place of improvement. That's where coaching really helps people. The benefit of an external coach is somebody comes in who is non-bias to the organisation. They're not playing political games. The thing with a mentor that's a little bit different is that they might be somebody in the company. Coaching, if done right, can really help somebody create that awareness and have that honest discussion. Because you already know the answers in your head, you just need to find the person to ask the right questions and make you accountable.

It's a journey.

Lee Eldridge in Summary

Characteristics of High Performers

- Consistency plays a huge role in everything they do.
- They understand what they need to focus on to shift the needle.
- They get a little bit better each day, session, or year.
- They optimise their day-to-day, week-to-week, and month-to-month.
- They are proactive reactives, meaning they activate core skills consistently.

How to Regain Control

- Create awareness of your lack of control.
- Identify who controls your diary.
- Carve out time during the day that is yours and that you control.
- Focus on your most important tasks during that time, ideally between 9-11 am.
- Start with 15-30 minutes and stretch out to 40 minutes or an hour.
- Understand how long you can concentrate, and aim for 100% concentration during that time.

Dealing with goals

- Understand that goals are for benchmarking and identifying progress. Don't let the failure to meet a goal demotivate you, but learn from it.
- Take the emotion out of the situation and use it as a learning experience.
- Use failures as motivation to try harder and strive for improvement.

On receiving feedback

- Develop a mindset that any feedback is helpful for your growth.
- Honesty is essential for a relationship to develop, even if it hurts.
- Feedback is lacking in business, so find people who will give you honest feedback.
- Stress has negative connotations, but it can also motivate us to improve. Use stress as a tool for growth and development rather than letting it overwhelm you.

- Develop coping mechanisms to manage stress, such as exercise or meditation.

How to contact Lee

My website is www.cognitveathlete.co.uk

You can find us on LinkedIn by looking up Lee Eldridge, and on YouTube, I've got some videos out there talking about sustaining high performance and a little bit about how to start your day. That's probably the best place for people to find out more about me and see what I'm up to.

Lee's Q&A

What's your version of success?

Everyone's version of success is different. My version is that I want to have the highest level of influence over the things I care about.

Top three books to read or listen to?

The 7 Habits Of Highly Effective People – Stephen Covey
The One Thing – Gary W. Keller and Jay Papasan
Backbone – David H. Wagner

What's your favourite quote?

"Success is not final; failure is not fatal: It is the courage to continue that counts."—Winston S. Churchill

What advice would you give your younger self?

Don't take yourself too seriously.

What is the best investment you have made, and why?

Myself, it's the only person that can get you out of the shit.

What's your go-to productivity trick?

Stop thinking that there are tricks!!

If you could write a book about your life, what would the title be and why?

Transformation over information – I am a learner, but in the past, I think that I needed to be more of a doer.

What's one thing you're learning now, and why is it important?

Research is the key to developing as a coach.

Who would you choose if you could trade places with anyone for a day?

Tiger Woods in the early 2000s. Unreal.

CHAPTER EIGHT

Michaela Wain

(Entrepreneurship)

About Michaela

Michaela is a BBC apprentice finalist, owner of Framework Marketing, Managing Director for Design and Build UK, Managing Director for Vantage Utility and Connections and Director for We Connect Construction. She is also a public speaker, podcast host, and mum of two.

In Michaela's own words:

I'm inspired by myself hearing that! I don't know how I find the time to do all of that, although I am really regimented and scheduled. Everything is planned for the day, and I have an amazing network to help me with my children. I've got fabulous teams within all of my businesses that run things when I can't be there. It's all about scheduling, funding, and being super organised.

My WHY

Steve: *I've made a history over the last 15 years by being process, procedure, borderline OCD, spreadsheet savvy and where everything's got its place. I think that's what's enabled me to be a little bit different in recruitment. I think people like us are both, as I call them, 'extended time people'. When you look at an individual, you think, "How are they doing all of this? Do they have the same number of hours as anyone else in the day? How do they do it? So, Michaela, how do you prioritise where you spend your time?*

Michaela: I mainly follow the money, to be honest. So, wherever I'm needed to bring money in is where I'm going to be. A lot of my companies are running themselves and have amazing directors and fabulous teams within them. I'll just sit on the board and step in when I need to, so I work on the businesses rather than within them and deal with strategic plans to scale, expand, exit, or whatever that might be at that time. I literally schedule time for my partner and my children. I know that sounds perhaps awful to people, but I have to do it. Every day between 5 pm and 7 pm, I will not use my phone and won't reply to people unless there is an emergency. During those times, I rarely reply to people, don't answer the phone, or don't do social media. Instead, I spend time cooking with the kids. Whatever happens, two hours every single day during the week are dedicated to my children because otherwise, if I never see them, then all of this is for nothing. Of course, realistically, there will be days if something major has to be dealt with around work, then it has to be dealt with, and that is what it is. But I consciously make an effort to ensure that my children have my full attention for those two hours because otherwise, they grow so fast, and you'll miss so much. For some folks, that scheduling time may be to exercise or whatever that might look like at this current time. I do things for myself as well because if I don't, then I'm not going to be productive at work, so I make sure that I do have that balance.

Delegation

Steve: *I often find there'll be people in a senior position who will struggle to delegate, outsource, and allow people the autonomy to do the role that they're employed to do. How have you managed that and enabled yourself to step away? Is it something you were always able to do?*

Michaela: I'm actually quite lazy, so I have made delegating a priority. I'm all about training people and want to employ leaders, not followers. I'd rather have somebody work for me for five years, who wants to learn from me and wants to grow themselves, and then they can go on and do their own thing; start their own business, for example. I need people who are going to be self-reliant, who are going to think outside the box, and who are going to educate themselves. I don't like to hear, "I don't like this," or "I can't do this". If they're struggling, I'd rather hear, "I'm unsure of this; can you help me?" or "Do you know how I can figure this out?" Rather than people who say, "I just can't do this". Those kinds of people aren't for me. It's difficult at first when people first come in, but we explain the culture of our companies; sometimes, people can feel like they're thrown into the deep end. But that's when you see if they will sink or swim.

Motivation

Steve: *How do you get the best out of people? What do you do to inspire others?*

Michaela: I don't know why people tell me I'm inspirational; I don't feel like I'm any different to anybody else. I suffer from imposter syndrome, and on a daily basis, I feel like I'm winging it. Then I have a reality check and think, "I've been doing this for 11 years – obviously, I know what I'm doing!".

I just believe if I can help somebody, then I will help them, and I will train people as best as I can. I think if you're a strong leader, you work hard, and people see that work ethic, then naturally, that motivates people. They think, "Oh god, she's grafting – I can't just sit here and do nothing because she's paying my wage!" I just work hard, help other people work hard, learn and develop themselves.

Mindset

My favourite saying by Winston Churchill is, 'When you're going through hell, keep going". I always remember that when I'm having a shitty time. The main thing I believe that helped my mindset be this way, of 'don't stop', is when I was younger. I was a middle-distance runner and long-distance for the age group that I was in. When you're in the middle of a field, and you've lost your shoes, and you're covered in shit, and everybody's running past you, then you think, "Oh my god, I've got to get up."

I used to represent the Northwest. So, the race would start well, but when the hills came, all the girls would start walking because we were knackered. I knew if I just used the chance on the hill where they were all walking, I was going to get to the front. So, when everybody else was flagging and struggling, that is when I would say to myself, "Right, now is the time. I'm just going to find the boost of energy from somewhere and take the lead there. Many people get that boost when they see the finish line, but I would wait for the most challenging part and take my chance there. I'm one of those vultures. My mum would be on the side-lines screaming, "If you don't walk in a winner, then you're going to be grounded'. That also motivates me. I had that mindset from being younger; I learnt the lesson that you need to dig deep if you're going to get there and achieve what you want to achieve. I really believe that that's helped me in business because I'm used to overcoming challenges.

I think everybody has got it in them. And the people who succeed in this world are the ones who don't stop. As soon as you stop, that's it. But if you do not stop, you do not give up, and you just keep on pushing through, you can do it.

If I went for a run tomorrow, I might get to five minutes and think, "I can't continue. It's -7 degrees, and my heart can't carry on."

But then I will think, "There's nothing physically stopping me. I've not just lost my leg. I can carry on!".

It's the same when it comes to business; there is nothing stopping you, or within your mind, there's nothing stopping you from thinking, "You know what, every single day, I'm going to reach out to 10 new prospects."

Then, over the course of the week, that's 50 people. Over the course of the month, that's 200 people, and from that, somebody is going to convert. So, when there are challenging times, set a small list of goals that you know you can achieve. If you start setting long-distance goals with ridiculous targets, things unachievable, your brain will start saying to you, "You failed."

Instead, set aside two hours to reach out to 10 people every day, and then, a month is going to come, and you're going to pat yourself on the back and say, "Yes, I did that." Then you'll slowly start seeing the return on these small things. So, when you are going through shit, and you're not really on track, you need to reduce those goals back, do something realistic and start taking baby steps again. Build yourself up because it could be a million this time next year!

Stop Negative Self-Talk

Stop beating yourself up, saying, "I can't do this, and I can't do that," we've got to be a bit kinder to ourselves. I firmly believe in scaling back those goals into bite-size realistic goals. Even if it's a 15-minute goal, just strip it back. Ask, "What can I actually achieve today to get into the routine of achieving things again?" Stripping it all back is what you can do. Then you become stronger and more confident in your ability, and then you can push the boundaries a little bit further.

Steve: *Exactly, and you become stronger as you become more confident in your own ability, and then you can push the boundaries that bit further.*

I made a note, as there was something in your bio that I picked up on. It resonates with me because I felt years ago, I was in a similar place. You talk about the fact that you have had social anxiety issues, going back some time, and the answer for you to help yourself was to go on The Apprentice, which has an average viewing figure of 5.8 million people. That seems like a drastic measure, so could you explain that to me?

Social Anxiety

When I was about 21, I was going through some shit and got really wrapped up in it all. From 21 to 25 it was really bad. I had six panic attacks a day, and at one point, I didn't leave my house for about six months. I had a chaotic life at the time, and many things were going on. Then I got pregnant with my son at 25 and realised that I had to turn my life around and start again better. But the panic attacks and anxiety would come and go in waves. I did all sorts of hypnotherapy and everything, but it was still there, coming and going.

My brother had been on Love Island, and I said to my mum, "Imagine if I was on the telly!" In the end, I got all the way to the end of The Apprentice, but it was very difficult. I have never sweated as much in my life as in those auditions to compete in that process. I was constantly this way for a period, and I've had one panic attack since then. When I feel panic, I think, "You know, I got fired by Lord Sugar – you can do anything, Michaela!"

That show is ruthless. I mean, you can see that from the viewer's perspective, but you don't get to see everything that goes on. It's ruthless, and you are there to be ridiculed, critiqued, torn apart, torn down, questioned, and reviewed. You're on a platform where people can just come and have a go if they want to, and I'd gone in there with all these worries, troubles, anxiety issues, and everything else. That's a phenomenal backbone.

Anything that's my weakness, I try and use it as a strength. I was so anxious during that show; how they got me talking in any scenes for the first couple of episodes was beyond me. I couldn't get the words out.

Before auditioning, I told them that I suffered from anxiety. I used my anxiety to my advantage. Lord Sugar felt sorry for me, and I wasn't one of these people that he would scream over in the boardroom. I was very good at sales when I was out and about on the street and wasn't in this high-pressure environment. And this got fed back to him – Claude really loved me. I'm still good friends with him now. He knew what I was capable of, so I didn't have to come in and talk myself up because I was just doing it. So, because of that, I think my shyness helped me throughout the process. I am just a bit of an idiot at times; I like to laugh in my life and don't take myself too seriously. We all make mistakes, and I can laugh and take the piss out of myself. I think that really helped me make loyal friends, which helped me throughout the full process, and what I deemed a weakness actually ended up being a strength.

If you have worries or concerns, you can learn to flip them so that they become the driver and the fuel to your fire.

Also, stop giving a shit about what everybody else thinks. My life has been so free since I've stopped worrying if people like me or if I say the right thing. You're human, and you're genuine, and as long as you're comfortable in who you are, what you do and what you say, then there's no right or wrong.

I think people see through the bullshit, and that's why brands are getting behind the person who owns the brand. It's about delivering on what you say you're going to deliver on. Don't promise the world but deliver on what you say you're going to deliver. That's a really important character trait and quite often lacking in sales. There are obviously a lot of people that are full of shit. But I just leave by being as honest as I can and say, "You know, I can't. I cannot promise you the world, but if I say I can do this for you, then I will fulfil what I say I'm going to do for you".

Then you get clients who become friends – a lot of my clients have been with us for the whole 11 years. And then clients who become friends become business partners. So just be nice; don't be a dick.

Role Models

Steve: *Over the years, so you've obviously met a lot of inspirational people, and I know you've interviewed some high-level elite people on the podcast, and you mingle with celebs. Are there two or three people that have genuinely inspired you? Who are the ones that stand out?*

Michaela: When I started in business, I didn't really have a role model. My parents are fabulous, but they weren't in business. I didn't really have anybody; then, it's only since The Apprentice that I realised how important mentors and coaches, inspirational figures, and surrounding yourself with people who are like us are. Since The Apprentice, my mindset has changed massively. The way I structure my business and how I work on my business have all completely changed because I'm just sucking information out of anybody and everybody who is more successful than me. Now there are several people. Firstly, Harrison, who is my partner. I met him on The Apprentice, and although we're not a lovey-dovey couple, he is a role model at this moment in time. I think your inspiration changes when you change in business. But Harrison is probably the most inspirational person because I see him all the time. Although we live apart, I speak to him more than anybody else. He constantly encourages me and knows where my weaknesses are in my business and personal life. He knows everything about me, and he will say, "Michaela, that's shit – you need to do this!" He introduces me to people, and he makes me feel good about myself. I feel pushed every single day. I think it's really important to have somebody who understands business and is willing to offer genuine feedback.

You have to find inspiration in people like Lord Sugar – he makes billions of pounds like that. He is levels and levels and levels ahead of me, which is great. I'm surrounded by people who are turning over a similar amount. Some people are turning over more than that, and others are turning over less. I think you need this equal split. I can talk you through what I've done. I can discuss with people where I'm at right now. And I can aspire to be like this person who's just a couple of levels ahead of me. I think it's important that you surround yourself with people in a similar circle to you.

Changing the Face of Construction

Steve: *I wanted to touch on one last thing, which is the fact that you're the Ambassador for Women in Construction. Surely that is a mammoth task; having myself worked in construction for 15 years recruiting professionals, I know it's a very male-dominated industry. Where did it come from?*

Michaela: Becoming Ambassador for Women in Construction was thrust upon me. To be honest, off the back of The Apprentice, I didn't even realise I was a woman in construction! I didn't know it was a thing. I've been very fortunate – I have been discriminated against, but it had never really registered with me. After the apprentice, I had hundreds of thousands of women getting in touch with me over the course of time, saying, "How do you deal with this? How do you deal with that? What's this?" I found I was advising women all the time. Then I started getting asked onto panels to do public speaking about it. Since then, I've heard the stories of so many amazing men in construction who acknowledged this issue but didn't know how to communicate it. I just thought, "You know what? I need to get involved here. Let's see if I can do something to bring the industry together."

I am 100% certain that I'm going to change this industry. I'm collecting people, directors of blue-chip companies, the CITB universities, colleges, and schools recruitment people, to take a roadmap to the government to regulate the construction industry. The roadmap is to ensure that by 2026, we will have got the industry from 13% women to 23% women, and instead of 1% on the tools, up to 5% on the tools. I want to make sure we can spread this down through the industry and not just one organisation. The key here is construction people look at themselves, thinking, "I want to lead the way!" It's really important that we use men to get our message across and do as much as we can to change this industry to attract women and decrease the skills gap shortage that will become increasingly worse due to Brexit. It's always been a candidate-led market, and there has always been a severe lack of good people in construction anyway.

I need everybody's help. Everybody in construction, on the cusp of construction, or remotely connected construction, I need your help. And all parents who aren't in construction, educate your children, please. This is not about digging holes on a construction site – you can be a quantity surveyor, an engineer, or you can be an architect. Women are capable of doing this too! I know women who do this on a daily basis, and it's loads of fun. There are lots of prospects, and there's lots of money. If you want your kids to be successful, consider construction.

In Summary

On-time management:

- Schedule your day and follow a regimented routine.
- Prioritise activities that generate revenue.
- Dedicate specific hours to personal activities, such as spending time with family or exercising.
- Ensure you have an amazing network to support you.

On delegation:

- Train and empower your team.
- Employ leaders, not followers.
- Encourage self-reliance and independent thinking.
- Delegate tasks to free up your time for more strategic planning.

On motivation:

- Work hard and set an example for your team.
- Help others develop and learn.
- Be a strong leader and inspire by example.

On mindset:

- Adopt a "don't stop" mentality.
- Embrace challenges and keep pushing forward.
- Remember the phrase, "When you're going through hell, keep going".

Finding Mentors and Role Models:

- Surround yourself with successful and inspirational people who can offer feedback and guidance.
- Seek out mentors and coaches who understand business and can help you improve.
- Look up to people who are several levels ahead of you in terms of success.

Breaking Gender Barriers in Construction:

- The construction industry is male-dominated, but there is a need to attract more women to address the skills gap shortage.
- Women can work in various roles in construction, including quantity surveyor, engineer, and architect.
- Parents should consider educating their children about the opportunities in construction to help break gender barriers.
- Michaela is leading an effort to increase the number of women in construction from 13% to 23% by 2026 and reduce the skills gap shortage. She is calling on everyone in or remotely connected to construction to help achieve this goal.

Contact Michaela.

I'm most active on LinkedIn and Instagram. On the LinkedIn app, I can't connect with people anymore, but you can follow me – I'm always checking my inbox. Same with Instagram. I'm super active on Clubhouse at the moment, so if you want a natural chat, get into Clubhouse and come to one of my rooms.

Email michaela@designandbuilduk.net
Website www.designandbuilduk.net
Socials are Michaela Wain.

Michaela's Q&A

What's your version of success?

Being able to provide for my children, work in an environment I enjoy, have control over my life and work the way I want to.

Top three books to read or listen to?

· Bloody Brilliant Women – Cathy Newman
· Make your Bed –William H. McRaven
· The Book You Wish Your Parents Read – Philippa Perry

What's your favourite quote?

"I have learnt over the years that when one's mind is made up, this diminishes fear; knowing what must be done does away with fear."

What advice would you give your younger self?

It will never be as bad as you fear; it will be much greater than you ever imagined.

What is the best investment you have made, and why?

Learning to understand investments, whether that is monetary or in myself and people. Understanding to wait things out, invest in the future and be patient. My older self has always been grateful for my younger self's efforts!

What's your go-to productivity trick?

Getting to the gym. If I don't go to the gym 4-5 times a week, my mind slowly starts to lose focus; I have learnt over the years that I work far more efficiently when I am training. I am one of those people who has to be active to be productive.

If you could write a book about your life, what would the title be and why?

Everything they never told you – I have read a lot of rubbish from 'gurus' over the years on business/life/parenting. I have listened to many talks and looked up courses, and there is so much waffle; I enjoy it when people tell the whole honest truth and stop faking it before they make it.

What's one thing you're learning now, and why is it important?

The importance of surrounding yourself with people who share your aspirations and drive. I believe it has held me back over the years, being unable to speak with people around me about business. When you talk about this in all conversations, you grow as a business owner, get ideas and clarity in those conversations, and unfortunately, not everyone wants to talk about business. I make sure I spend time with people who can help me grow and learn.

Who would you choose if you could trade places with anyone for a day?

My boyfriend, so I can have the pleasure of spending a full day with me! Haha – just kidding. I would probably like to be a man in a successful company like Bill Gates and watch how people treat him. I am interested in people's reactions to people and how they change themselves.

CHAPTER NINE

Mike Ames

(Recruitment)

About Mike

M ike has built and sold two recruitment businesses from scratch, with a turnover at point of sale of £40,000,000 and £24,000,000, respectively, with a combined total sale value of £39,000,000. He now works with small and micro recruitment firm owners who want to build a better lifestyle and be financially secure. This can be achieved by building a scalable business based upon seven pillars that create a solid foundation for growth called a Factory Model. You can use a Factory with 360s, but creating a Layered Fulfilment function is considerably safer.

In Mike's own words:

Steve: *Why do you feel people have nominated you to be on The Guestlist Podcast?*

Mike: I think there are two reasons; first of all, I spent about £250 bribing people to put my name forward because I was so keen to come on the show. But, in all seriousness, I think it's because I have a track record. There are a lot of people out there that are choosing consultants in the space, but they've never actually done it themselves. You know, even people who've been successful in big companies, that's not the same as sitting around your dining room table and saying, "We can do this; we can start and build a business". Then having to go through the phases of your development along with all the trials and tribulations of running a business. Lastly, you have the exit, perhaps a sale. I'm telling you that is not an easy experience to navigate. To do that once is unusual to do it twice is very unusual. And I think perhaps that gives me a different space to occupy.

One of the things that I've been a big believer in is collaboration, and I don't try to look where there's conflict or competition, although that, of course, exists, and in many cases, you can't ignore it. But instead, look at people and see how you can collaborate and help because you'll get a lot more from that.

We always had a network back in the day, and you knew who the competition was. I think there were more "big names" in recruitment in those days because people got paid more, so it attracted bigger beasts. We all knew each other, and everyone went out for drinks, and you would let a little bit go, and then you get a little bit back. But the deal was that if you saw your competitor drowning, you threw stones at them (and then went for a beer afterwards). Now, it's much more collaborative, which I think is considerably better too.

What do you feel separates the average from the high-level performance?

If I would distil it down, I'd probably say three things. The first one must be focus. We have a saying, 'Concentrate to penetrate, penetrate to accumulate'. It's a new business thing; if you want to be successful, focus on less because you'll achieve more. And I think anyone who achieves a lot is focused. The question isn't, 'CAN I do that?' The question is, 'SHOULD I do that?' And they're very different questions. For example, you can quite easily take on a different type of vacancy or stray into a new sector, but is that right for you? Often it isn't because it weakens your focus and so means you achieve less.

When Bill Gates was having lunch with Warren Buffett, his dad was there to organise the lunch. Bill Gates's Dad said, "You know, I've got the two richest men in the world sitting in front of me having lunch. That's got to be unusual. Why do you think you're so successful? Why are you so rich?" So, he got them to write down one word on a piece of paper separately and asked them to show it at the same time. Guess what word that was? It was focus!

If you get a moment, Google 'Jony Ive and Steve Jobs – focus' – the best way to spend 93 seconds I can think of.

The second success factor is to be very organised. Speaking as someone who's dyslexic, I have memory problems, and I can't remember sequences very well. So, I've had to develop coping strategies around organisation; I might not be very talented, but I am very organised, and that organisation has made up for my weaknesses in other areas. Organised people have a system to capture and manage tasks so they don't forget anything, rely heavily on their CRM system, and make notes that they can easily find when they want them. You just need to develop a system that works for you and stick to it. Do that, and you'll significantly increase your chances of success.

Finally, your work ethic has a lot to do with your chances of success, but perhaps not in the way you think. I've known plenty of talented people that are lazy. The other day, I did an episode of the mind game show on how 'being lazy is good for you'. I don't mean work-shy; I just mean always looking for ways to do things quicker, easier, and better. But I think laziness is not a good thing when it equates to work shyness.

You've got to put the hours in the grafting to get to where you need to be. The trick, is to build a business so other people do that for you.

JC Penney, the American retail magnate, once said, "The most seminal moment in my business career was when I discovered I couldn't do it all myself", and neither can you.

What leader's traits enable growth of a business?

I've held this view for years and tried to live up to it as best as possible. Three things. There's a lot of overlap between management and leadership, but they're very different. I think as a leader, you have three main jobs to do. The first one is to make your people truly fabulous at what they do. That means understanding their strengths and weaknesses as people, not rushing them through training courses, but really getting to know them, mentoring, coaching, and investing in them. It means equipping them with the right tools and materials they might need to do their job and setting everything up so that if they're the striker, the whole team is about them putting a goal in the back of the net. It should almost be an obsession to help everybody in your team reach mastery of what they do. I always wanted everybody to be better than me because I'm only an average recruiter, truth be told. I was never that brilliant. And most people I hired were better than me, which suited me down to the ground.

I think the second thing is you've got to make sure everyone's happy. It's so important. And to do that, you must understand what motivates each of your people, what frightens them, what's happening in their lives, and what they want to achieve. You also must recognise that nobody stays with you forever. You're a custodian of those people; they work for you, so it's your job to help them during that period. They will most probably go somewhere else and do something else, and you'll be helping to do that. Weirdly, the more you understand that, the less likely they are to leave.

Thirdly, you must give people a mission, which is a reason and a purpose to go to work which is more than just to earn money. The people who get behind your mission are the kind of people who will stay with you and do their best. Those people who are just focused on the money will go somewhere else if they are offered more money, or they'll go and set up on their own. If you want a team of people who will build your empire for you, you need a stable team who believes in the mission.

Those three things drive the way that you are with people. It drives initiatives within the firm; it drives focus. It also means you've got to have a purpose and a strategy, and a plan. So, a whole bunch of things stem from those three things. And I personally think when I've worked for leaders in the past, those three things have been there in spades.

When I used to recruit into my companies, I never sold a job; I sold a mission and a culture. From the get-go, I'd say, "This is what we're trying to achieve. This is what we want to be known as, and this is how it's going to work. This is the plan to achieve that."

You're dead in the water if you're a leader and don't believe you're on a mission. Everyone I interview is good at what they do, so we're not even talking about that. What we are talking about is, "Do you share my values? Do you want this mission? Because if not, you're not coming." And that's how you keep a business on track.

The biggest lesson in Business Growth

Steve: *So, throughout the two companies' growth, I imagine there's been lots of ups and downs. There have been huge wins and areas where things haven't worked. What would you say was perhaps the biggest failure or the biggest lesson?*

Mike: So, when we started, there were three of us, and I was the least experienced in terms of sales. The guy that ran it was my ex-agent when I was a freelancer, then my boss when I first went into recruitment, and then he became my business partner. He was an outstanding person and a massive influence on me, but he tragically died in a car crash. He was killed 18 months into the business, and so I was in charge with no clue what I was doing. So, I did what I always do in those circumstances; I threw time at it. I'm very determined, and I won't let things go, and I just keep going and falling over and getting back up again. Eventually, we had this upsurge mostly through the work he'd done before he died. But then I started to believe my own publicity and thought that more of our success was down to me than it was.

Nothing moved in that business without me, and in small businesses, you can do that, but it's not scalable. Then three things happened within days of each other: a sort of nervous breakdown, big problems in my marriage, and a business that had stopped growing. It suddenly made me realise that having been one of the business's big assets, I was now easily its biggest liability. I began to realise that the business needed to depend less on me to scale. That was the biggest thing I learnt. And it's a really big thing because everyone knows that everyone talks about it, but then you've got to do things which make it happen, and that's not so easy because you're basically saying, "I'm not as important as I thought I was. I've got to trust people to do things and not be involved in what they do. I've got to have people fail and watch them fail and know they're going to fail. It's necessary because it's part of their development, and I need to do that." That was hard.

Luckily, we hired a coach who helped us through this process and had a big effect on me personally. She got me to transition so that I no longer saw the business as the Mike Ames show. It wasn't a failure in the sense that we carried on, but it was a personal failure and could have ended in disaster.

And, in the mind of a leader, you must allow people to fail because that's when they learn. If you think about it, most of us walk around now because we fell over a lot when we were toddlers, but we got up and fell over trying to walk the first few times. That's what failure does.

Winston Churchill said, "It's not how many times you fall down; it's how many times you get up that counts."

How to Become a Top Biller

Steve: *We've got a wide range of listeners/readers, including people that are just embarking on their recruitment journey and not yet having set foot in the office, and there are experienced people who are doing great. However, anybody that comes into this line of work will always dream of being the top performer, the highest biller, with the ability to go and make financial choices down the line. What advice would you give people that are starting the journey with dreams of being the top performer or the high biller?*

Mike: I think the first piece of advice applies to everybody, no matter what you do, and that is to invest in yourself. You have to decide early on whether you want this thing you're doing to be a job or a profession. Because if it's a job, you can just rock up in the morning, do your thing, and go home. Nothing special, but you do your job and earn your money.

Very few people can just be successful by relying on their talent and good looks – you need mastery, so invest in yourself continually. A day you don't learn is a wasted day – it's crucial, and you can do that in lots of ways. Back in the day, you had to go on courses. These days it's different. We have the internet and YouTube, and people are giving courses away all over the place. Learning what you need to learn is easy, and you can do many things. I don't think it's access to the content that's important.

My advice is to create a mentality that says, "If I invest in myself, whether it's in the company's time or my own time, I'm the one who gains the most from it. I may stay at this company for a long time, or I may not, but every time I learn something and get better at something, it's worth it". If you believe in marginal gains as I do, you just need to get a little bit better, many times over, to be awesome at what you do.

But there's a big bear trap that any of us can fall into. You reach a stage of competency and think, "I've got this", so you stop learning and investing in yourself. My advice is don't do this. I continue to learn daily; I spend between 30 to 60 minutes a day exposing myself to new things, mostly from Twitter, Blinkist and YouTube. I usually do this whilst I'm eating breakfast or lunch.

By the way, I'm a big Blinkist fan. I don't know whether you've come across it, but you can read a book in 20 minutes, and I consume an enormous amount of content that way. Sometimes I'll then buy the actual book because I think it's a good one to have, and I want to read it properly.

I also listen to a lot of podcasts and audiobooks in the car. I want to mentally feed myself with new content, and then I can sift out the things I want to adopt for myself.

The second piece of advice for recruiters' is don't just focus on the commission at the end of the month. Even though your business and the people who employ you have probably structured things that way. Regardless of what they say, they want you to hit gross profit at the end of the month, and that's what's most important to them. Well, it's important to you, of course, but other things are important as well.

For example, developing long-term relationships with clients, prospects, contractors, and intermediaries is massively important, but you can't do that in a month. You've got to do things now, which may pay out in six, nine or 12 or even 18 months' time. If you're obsessed entirely by the end of the month, you won't do what you need to do to create those relationships and build your empire for you.

You've got to develop the skills and experience to do what we call Tactical BD – vacancy scraping and candidate speccing. Very important if work is starting to dry up, but if that's all you do, that's all you'll ever do, which is very hard work. You need a series of high-value clients; by the way, I don't mean high volume.

High-value clients value their suppliers, want to work with them, are open to building a close working relationship, will pay what you are worth and have a steady stream of vacancies you can fill. Imagine adding another two clients a year to your client estate who are like your very best client – what a difference would that make?

By the way, that Hunter Killer thing where you get a vacancy, then turn your attention to filling the vacancy and start again isn't scalable, and it certainly doesn't make exponential growth very easy.

You need a Strategic BD strategy alongside your Tactical BD activities. One that will target high-value clients over a much longer period. That's how you win more high-value clients, and each time you do, you add another layer of revenue on top of the last one you won. That's how you grow it to £40 million or £60 million because the vacancies are coming to you now, not the other way around.

I think if you just want to be a jobbing consultant, whether it's your own business or somebody else's is fine, you know, go and hunt a vacancy, and then fill it. Absolutely fine. But if you want to grow a scalable business, you've got to see it differently; you must win more high-value clients.

Compound Effect and 1%

Steve: *I went through a period where I bought all the consultants that I recruited or who worked with me a copy of The Compound Effect by Darren Hardy, which is a great book. Anybody that hasn't looked at the compound effect or the 1% incremental changes needs to read about Dave Brailsford. How have you implemented that philosophy?*

Mike: These things are massive to me, not only as an individual but for your business too. The first thing to do is accept that you've got weaknesses, and your business has weaknesses, too, but many people don't like doing that. I mean, you have to seek them out, and that's not easy because we all want the things that we create to be good. You know, we don't want to create something that's got malfunctions about it. So, I advise reaching out to your clients and saying, "I'd like you to tell me what we do well". We can keep doing what you like, but I'm much more interested in what we do wrong.

There's this thing called VOTC, 'voice of the customer', which we also use for ourselves and our clients. It's such an interesting thing because what it does is encourage criticism. You'll be amazed how difficult it is for me to convince some of our clients to go ahead and do a VOTC program, even though I can prove that it pays for itself. Nobody wants to say, "I've not done this as well as I could have done". But that's where true greatness lies.

You're looking for systematic faults in your people and your business, and VOTC will find these for you. You can also ask your employees and suppliers to because they always know how you could be better. Just like you know how your clients could be better. But no one asks, do they?

So, you collect the feedback, analyse it and decide what you're going to implement and what you're not going to implement. Then report back to the source to say, "You know, that thing you told us? Great, we did it. It's brilliant. Thank you for that."

I was talking to a German businessman once who'd worked in England. He said, "In Germany, in many of the companies I've worked for, quality is the first thing on the agenda – not the numbers. The second thing is innovation. Always asking, "How good are we, and how can we get better?" He said in England, those things are hardly mentioned, or they tack it onto the bottom of a meeting."

I looked at him and thought, without knowing it, I've always believed that quality was important to me. So is innovation to change and experiment and see if what you change may be better or worse, or no difference at all, and continually do that. It's inevitable that you'll bubble to the top. It's inevitable; it's unshakable. So, if you want to be successful, it's there for you. It's not rocket science. It's more of a change of mentality and then the discipline to implement things that you learn more than anything else.

I like the word criticism. I don't even care about constructive criticism. And you don't have to tell me how I can make it better or give me a criticism sandwich. Because when I've got to the emotional setback where I've been told that I'm not as good as I thought I was, and then faced with the possibility to improve, tell me and criticise me.

Who are your biggest influences?

My father was one. I could talk about him for the rest of this interview. He was full of flaws, wasn't educated, and was dyslexic like me. He was dyslexic at a time that people didn't understand it, and it built up into frustration. But he gave me a belief in myself, and he was entrepreneurial but didn't take risks. So, he knew what to do and what he wanted to do, but he couldn't do it. And I realised that I needed to take risks if I was going to be successful. What makes people rich is what they are prepared to sacrifice and how many risks they take. So, he was the one that helped me to get around that and supported me in everything that I did.

In terms of business, I think there are two people: one was Mike Sparkes, my business partner, who died. I'm not saying this because he's dead, and we remember the dead fondly, but he was awesome. He was the best recruiter I knew, the best relationship manager. He had faults, but he was just brilliant. He mentored me and put me on the road to success. He believed in me. He offered me the job to get into recruitment. I hadn't thought about it. He said, "I think you'd be a good recruiter". How wrong was he? But he was brilliant, and he was transitional in my life.

The other person is whom I mentioned when I had a near nervous breakdown when we weren't scalable, and I was the problem. I hired a consultant. Her name was Anne Marie Hanlon. She was brilliant because she taught me what scalability looked like. And I've been teaching people that ever since because the principles of scalability are pretty simple. The things you need to do in order to be scalable are not rocket science. She made me see those basic principles. She worked with us for about 18 months. During that period, she completely transitioned me to realising it was my job to make my people fabulous at what they did, happy in their work, and give them a mission that we can all get behind, and then to organise a business to make that happen. She taught me that and was massively influential on me, and more so than she'd ever know, probably.

Progress

Have you heard the expression, 'You can't make a butterfly by making a caterpillar fatter?' And it's true – the caterpillar becomes a chrysalis so it can transform itself, and then it becomes a butterfly. It's the same in businesses; you get to a certain stage, you need to reform it, and then it can grow into the next stage.

It's called the 3, 7 and 15 rule. Three years to create a viable business, another four to make it scalable, and finally, eight years to make yourself independently wealthy.

So, if you've just started your business, first of all, don't worry too much about what's going to come. Secure your revenue streams, go on Steve Guest's course, figure out how to get that business coming in, and you know how to get when your clients and put your bum on the seat. But never lose sight from day one that you are no longer a recruiter who owns a business but rather a businessperson who happens to do recruitment. There's a world of difference between the two.

Another thing about the businessperson mentality is to 'start with the end in mind'. Ask yourself, what's the exit going to be? You have two options. The first is a Cash-Cow-Lifestyle business where you generate a lot of profits but not much value. You then take the profit out each year, invest it privately, and buy property, stocks and shares. So, each year, you are becoming progressively more wealthy and aren't killing yourself doing it.

Alternatively, you can build a Scale-4-Sale business that you intend to sell one day. They're different beasts but remember, in the UK, only 0.2% of all recruitment companies are ever sold in a commercial trade sale.

In any event, make your decision and go for what you need. The more you focus on that, the more likely you are to achieve it within your desired timeframes. Personally, I'd go for a Cash-Cow-Lifestyle business model because you'll have a better quality of life and are massively more likely to be rich one day.

One single piece of advice

Build relationships, don't chase vacancies. Create a Strategic BD function in your company that wins high-value clients so the vacancies come to you, and you don't need to chase them. If you don't fancy this (Lord help us), you can spend some time defining what an ideal client looks like for you, then go on to LinkedIn, find 20 of them, and stick them in a spreadsheet. Then just focus on those buggers until they become clients, or at least some do. That's going to take your time. You're not going to make money out of them this month, next month, this year, maybe who knows, but you will make money out of them one day and hopefully a lot of money in the future.

Mike Ames in Summary

- Invest in yourself by building a track record and gaining experience in your industry.
- Collaborate and help others to get more out of your connections.
- Focus on less to achieve more. Concentrate to penetrate, penetrate to accumulate.
- Focus on the right things by asking yourself, "Should I do this?" instead of "Can I do this?"
- Develop coping strategies to compensate for weaknesses.
- Make your people truly fabulous at what they do by mentoring, coaching, and investing in them.
- Ensure everyone is happy by understanding what motivates and frightens them and what they want to achieve.
- Recognise that nobody stays with you forever, and be a custodian of your people by helping them even after they leave.
- Accept your weaknesses and seek them out actively to improve your business.
- Use VTC (Voice of the Customer) programs to encourage criticism and identify potential improvements in your business.
- Look for systematic faults within your business and fix them.
- Quality and innovation should be the first things on the agenda of a successful business.
- Embrace criticism and feedback, even if it is not constructive.
- Take risks if you want to be successful in business.
- Believe in yourself and surround yourself with supportive people who believe in you.
- Focus on making people happy and give them a mission to get behind.

- Organise your business to make your mission happen.
- Implement the basic principles of scalability to grow your business.

Contact Mike

Email: mike.ames@recruitmentpioneers.com
Website: https://www.recruitmentpioneers.com/
LinkedIn: https://www.linkedin.com/in/mspames/

Mike's Q&A

What's your version of success?

To have the time and money to do what I want, when, where, and with whom I want. And for as long as I want.

Top three books to read or listen to?

Purple Cow by Seth Godin
How to Win Friends and Influence People by Dale Carnegie
Outliers by Malcolm Gladwell

What's your favourite quote?

"Nothing in this world can take the place of persistence. Talent will not; nothing is more common than unsuccessful men with talent. Genius will not; unrewarded genius is almost a proverb. Education will not; the world is full of educated derelicts. Persistence and determination alone are omnipotent. The slogan 'Press On!' has solved and always will solve the problems of the human race." Calvin Coolidge, 30th President of the USA.

What advice would you give your younger self?

Give more time to your family.

What is the best investment you have made, and why?

The best investment I made by a country mile is the time I have spent in personal self-development in a wide range of skills, tools and techniques. The Return On Investment (ROI) on that is incalculable.

What's your go-to productivity trick?

Start work at 5 am, and the first thing I do is plan out the day.

If you could write a book about your life, what would the title be and why?

Mike Who? Because that's how we all start off in business – it's down to you to let the world know who you are.

What's one thing you're learning now, and why is it important?

How to launch online products because that will be our business's future.

Who would you choose if you could trade places with anyone for a day?

If it was anybody in history, I'd say David Niven in the 30s, and today it would have to be Bryson DeChambeau – just to make one drive over 400 yards!

CHAPTER TEN

Simon Thorpe

(Leadership / Recruitment)

About Simon

Simon Thorpe is an experienced performance development specialist and behaviour change psychologist. Simon has made significant contributions to individuals, teams and organisations in business, sports, education and voluntary sectors. Formerly an accomplished athlete, Simon's speciality is inspiring his audience to improve performance by igniting the potential that lies within us all and has the passion for enabling others to further improve their performance. He's trained in motivational interviewing, positive psychology and cognitive behavioural coaching. Simon has designed and delivered workshops and programs in various settings; government agency recruitment, commerce, medical education, health and care, leisure, hospitality, manufacturing, and at a range of levels regionally, nationally, and internationally. He is referred to as a thought leader in the subject of leadership, management, and, more recently, happiness and well-being. Simon regularly contributes to articles and debates, as well as organisation strategy and implementation, thought and action-provoking delivery in front of small or multinational audiences. Whether public speaking training or facilitating, Simon's style is engaging, inspirational, and realistic. Working all over the world, Expressions has enjoyed having unique solutions presented on the international stage and awarded a national scholarship to America. Simon has studied at the University of Florida College for Medicine, Health and Human Performance and holds leadership positions in business education and sport.

In Simon's Own Words:

What are the key traits that separate high performers from anyone else?

Steve: In your experience, what would you say are perhaps some of the key traits that separate high performance from anyone else?

Simon: Fundamentally, it's mindset. It's the approach you take to a situation. It's having that resilience, that mental toughness, to deal with the situations that you're faced with. So, if it's, for example, a professional athlete who wants to improve their performance in an event, a sport, or a tournament, it's saying, "I've got to do whatever it takes to make sure I achieve that potential". If it's someone in the sales business, for example, 1001 obstacles could get in the way and probably will get in the way. So, the first thing I'll say is to be mindful of what obstacles might hinder you from achieving what you want. Say there are five top obstacles that could get in the way. From a behaviour change perspective, we then say, "And if that were to happen, what could you do?" So, you're forewarned and prepared for if that happens. My team and I call it 'what ifness?'. "What if that happened? What else could you do?" It's being prepared for any eventuality that happens and not allowing external factors to knock you completely off your track. It might deviate you from your track, but it's okay. Things happen, and we can get around it. Then you need the grit to keep doing it. I remember once reading a quote; one of my childhood heroes was Daley Thompson, a decathlete. The quote was, 'I always train on Christmas Day because not many people do.' It's about doing something that other people aren't doing. If you want to be the best in your field, you can learn from people who you look up to, admire and respect and then do something just that little extra. I'm not saying work 20 hours a day; I'm saying work eight, but make sure they are good.

Stress

Steve: *I think we'll always find excuses and reasons not to do something or justify why we've decided not to do something. I quite often find myself saying, "It is what it is". I think you have to become accepting that you can't deal with everything. You can't change certain things, and you've got to face it head-on and deal with it in a positive way. I think the more times I find myself saying, "It is what it is", I feel more relaxed, more on a level, and think okay, "So, what do I do now? Where do I go?" How do you feel about that?*

Simon: We work with individuals, teams and managers on the subject of stress because it's a big topic. What we have found is there are two particular camps of coping. There are problem-focused coping and emotion-focused coping. From a very simplistic perspective, what if you were caught in traffic on the M25, or whatever traffic route you normally take, and you think, "I can't go forwards, backwards or sideways." You look around at people who are caught in similar traffic, and some people are losing their stuff – effing and jeffing using, shall we say, nonverbal communication hand signals. Now, what is that actually doing? You can't fix the problem. I can't move my car, and I can't move other cars out of my way. Therefore, I've got to use emotion focus coping. I can't fix this, but what can I fix? Can I have a hands-free phone call to the person I'm going to meet? Or to my colleagues and family and say, "Hey, guess what? I'm on the M25. Sorry, I'm stuck here. Shall we have the meeting now? I'm hands-free in the car." "Are you okay with delaying by 30 minutes?" "My eta is about 30 minutes later, or do we reschedule?"

That's an emotion-focused coping way of doing something. What if you had a falling out with a colleague at work yesterday? Can I fix that problem? I probably can by saying to the colleague, "Steve, in the cold light of day, my apologies. I said some things I didn't really mean yesterday. I'm sure you probably did the same thing. Can we iron out this crease before it becomes a tear?"

So, you can fix the problem. But if you can't fix a problem, you fix your approach to the problem. There's a concept known as 'problems, and problems about problems.' For example, having a sleepless night is probably not the problem. Is your mind occupied by the fact that you're falling short of your targets this month? That's the actual problem, and the sleeplessness is a problem *about* the problem. Which do you think is more common? The problems, or the problems about the problems?

You got it, the latter. We're focusing on dealing with the problems about the problems and not really fixing or dealing with the problem itself. So, we're constantly going to be treading water or fighting against many different barriers and things that get in the way. That's why we don't always perform as well as we can, because we're not fixing the absolute root cause.

I was doing an inset day at a school about resilience. I put a slide on the PowerPoint and said, "Here's a phrase you've probably heard many times and probably used yourselves many times." The phrase was, 'I'll worry about that later'. So, I asked, "Why are you going to worry about it later?"

What you mean is you're delaying the worry.

The words we say to ourselves have the most impact on us. So rather than saying, "I'll worry about that tomorrow", I say, "I'll deal with that tomorrow, or I'll manage that better later." Words have a lot of power.

Happiness

We run a 'Happy Workshop' and are the first organisation to do so in the UK. I first say to the audience, "I greeted all of you this morning, and I've asked you how you are. Most of you answered, "Yeah, not too bad". I said, "Not too bad? So normally, does your life absolutely suck, but today, it's just not as bad?" What I meant was, "Say what you mean!" You can say, "Actually, I'm doing alright!" but don't lie and say, "I feel amazing," if you don't. Instead, you can say, "Yeah, I'm managing life. I'm getting on with things and looking forward to today."

Our mindset is usually about getting through the day. Let's be clear, occasionally, that's going to happen – we're all human beings, we're fallible, we have issues, and we have things we've got to deal with. But if that becomes your modus operandi, once a week, once a month, one week every month, that's not a great place to be. It's a habit. And habits are formed when we do things again. The most recent research suggests that it takes, on average, 66 days to change a habit.

For example, in January, we're littered with people who are saying, "New year, new me – here we go. I'm gonna join the gym, do running and yoga and go on the cabbage soup diet." (Please don't ever do the cabbage soup diet – it's not good for the people around you!) Instead, you should commit to something and see it happen. The same thing applies to work goals and high-performance goals.

Quiet Goals

People often share their goals on social media, but I would advise against that. Don't share your goals with too many people. If you announce that you're going to run a marathon and achieve 300k in earnings a month, you'll hear a lot of praise and adulation, and you've already gotten some validation from an external source, and you think you're doing really well, which might make you lose the motivation to actually achieve the goal. Instead, ask those close to do you a favour.

Ask them if they could check in with you once a month. "Ask me how I'm doing on my goals." Therefore, there's a commitment with someone else. "I won't let you down. I won't let myself down."

You must have the commitment to keep moving forwards, but first of all, keep moving, and ideally, keep moving forward.

If you really want to do something, do it – no one's going to do it for you. Sure, draw upon help, assistance, guidance, and coaching from external sources, but do what you said you're going to do. You made a commitment to yourself, and now the only person you're letting down is you. That concerns me if you're okay with that because you're saying you're not important enough. Whether you're a manager or recruiter, in any sector, in any business, if you're a family person, a father, mother, a brother or a sister and aunt and uncle, you have made a commitment. So, honour that commitment.

Do what you say you're going to do. Many years ago, I was told a definition of integrity. And many people say they have integrity, but when asked what it means, they will say 'honesty'. Actually, integrity is defined as.

"Doing what you say you're going to do,
even when you're not being watched".

It's that last bit that's important. I said I would do it. Therefore, I'm going to own that commitment. I will do it because I promised you and myself.

It's about the perspective of failure. Not many people like failing, and that's understandable. But how do you know if you're succeeding if you haven't failed? You have to fail to learn to get better. It's all part of resilience. Being more resilient doesn't mean bad things don't happen to you; it simply means you can better manage them. I personally believe in bouncing forwards, not bouncing back. If you bounce back, you go back to your original dimension, shape, and form, but bouncing forwards means 'I've gained something from this situation'. 'That was a massive failure point for me, but actually, I've now learnt that didn't work. Therefore, I can now do this. And you can apply that to a golf swing, a sales conversation, managing individuals, running your business, or writing a book. Of course, if you make the same mistakes more than twice, then something's not being learnt, but we must celebrate every single experience.

One thing I talk a lot about, especially in recruitment, sales, and management, is every single day before you clock off or log off your system, just spend a few minutes either individually or with your team and say, "What have I actually achieved today?" That's not about how many emails you sent or how many meetings you attended, but what you actually achieved and why it was an achievement. You may also reflect on what didn't go so well. Then consider how you can be better tomorrow.

We have an inherent fear of failure that comes from pressures from peers, pressures from parents and families and is an inherent point of our academic system. If you get bad grades in maths, that tends to infiltrate your mind to think, "Maybe I can't do any job that requires problem-solving, mathematical ability, calculating or working things out. Therefore, I'll go and become a sportsperson." (You've got to work those things out being a sports person, actually! But it's very limiting. So, in the growth mindset, the teacher will say, "Simon, you're not good at maths YET. But we'll find a way where you can become better. I'm not suggesting you'll be a mathematician, or a maths teacher or an accountant in your future, but you will be able to master a part of this maths and become better at doing it."

But the fundamental thing is, as humans, we typically have an average of a nine-to-one negativity bias, which means we are more predisposed to think of the negative over the positive. The nine-to-one negativity bias is born out of our prime motivation for self-survival and self-preservation, and it hasn't evolved too well within our brains since we were cavemen. Now, it's become worse because we play those movies of the worst-case scenario in 3D and Surround Sound in our heads. A part of the brain – the amygdala says, "Don't do that. Yeah, that's going to go really bad. No, no, really bad. Remember the 'What ifness' from earlier? "What if that were to happen? What could you do?"

So that the whole thing is paying attention to what's going on in your brain, and then the rest of it follows suit, be it good, bad or ugly.

Perspective

Steve: *I was always the reserved, quiet, unassuming type who didn't take any risks and didn't want to put myself out there. I think the turning point for me was having children, going to work, doing things for someone else, and allowing them to have greater opportunities as they grow up. So, my view became that I would take all the risks head-on; I'll hit things first because I want to be able to pass on life lessons, business lessons, whatever they might be to my boys. Now, I'm more willing to fall flat on my face and fail every day because I don't necessarily want my boys to go through that. But I'll still tell them to go and give it a go, even if they don't succeed because it's helped me. I think the more things I can do and the more prepared I am, the better person I've become. It's a journey. So bad day to a good day, tomorrow, bad shot at golf, it's just one of many shots. A bad trade, if I'm trading, is just one trade.*

Simon: Absolutely, you have to put the wins and losses into perspective. Ask yourself, 'Does this one trade affect my life?' 'Does this client opportunity affect my life?' 'Does this one success fulfil my life?' Probably not. Think of your life as a box set. Every box set has got a dodgy episode, doesn't it? Thus, occasionally, we have a dodgy episode or a pretty weak storyline. So, think of your life as a massive box set and that the story will go incredibly well along the journey, but you create the script along the way. And if you want to have a fantastic ending for that box set, change the script along the way. Make sure it's the best storyline possible.

Comparison

The biggest challenge of happiness is comparison. If I'm comparing myself with you, I feel I have to be as good as you, or how I perceive how good you are, and then I'd constantly never be happy with who I am and what I'd achieved. So, I'm massively in favour of ambition, high performance, and being the best that you could be, but be happy.

In sales-type organisations, you're on a monthly commission structure many times, sometimes quarterly, and what happens in the month if you achieve the target? Next month, your target is now plus 10%. This happens at the annual appraisals – you must hate those things. "You've had a fantastic year; well done, you've achieved your £1,000,000 target. I'm so impressed. Well done. So next year, it's going to be £1,020,000." Now, so that adulation, that praise, that recognition, that appreciation for 365 days of work is less than one minute before you get another target.

I would ask that salesperson, "How did you achieve that million pounds? What is it you did? What actions did you take?"

"Well, I've got up at five o'clock in the morning."

"Okay, did that work for you?"

"Well, yeah."

"Great. We're now going to build your success formula. What you've done in the last year, could you apply to the coming year to continue that success principle?"

Otherwise, you're starting from zero again.

Many people don't feel they can press pause and look at how they've done what they've done and why they've done it. All too often, we say, "Oh, I haven't got time for that. I'm so busy." But ask, what are you busy doing? Busy going in the wrong direction? Busy duplicating effort? Busy making mistakes and not recognising them? Often, it's about having the discipline to press pause for a moment and say, "Wait a minute, let's check my compass. Am I still going in the right direction?"

Analysing is about pressing pause to think about what's working and not working. I do a New Year's Goals exercise. It's not just writing goals; it has four quadrants. The first quadrant is what successes I have experienced in the last year. That can be personal, social, and professional. The second box asks, "What unsuccessful experiences did I have?"

Always start with the positive. Otherwise, you go back to the nine-to-one negative bias. And the third box, I think, is the most important box. 'Lessons Learned'. "What have I learnt about that?" I learnt that if I get up and exercise in the morning, my day is beautiful for the rest of the day." "If I don't fulfil the commitments I make to myself, I beat myself up." These are lessons to learn. The fourth quadrant is your goals for the coming year, personal, professional and financial. You can customise it how you like, but spend that bit of time asking "why did that work?"

I go into organisations, especially recruitment organisations, and I ask, "When's the last time you met with your team just to focus on why it was so good last month?"

You can be assured there will be a meeting with the team if things have gone badly in the previous month and someone's going to get fired. However, it's called 'appreciative inquiry' if it's going really well. "Why did that work?" not "Was it a fluke?"

You're building your success formula by looking at what you did right. If you can replicate and scale that, whether it's an individual running a desk, a team, a division, or a whole company, focus on your success principles and just work the hell out of them because it's working for you.

How to find what motivates you

Steve: *A few weeks ago, I was asked by a consultant, "I really don't feel motivated today. What can I do to get over this hurdle?"*

I said, "Okay, well, just answer this question. Why are you doing what you do?"

"Oh, you've put me on the spot a little bit there." He said.

"I mean, why are you doing what you do? Why are you getting up every morning to go to work? To do what you do?"

I sent him away to think and rethink what is 'the why' that motivates and moves him to get up every morning and be successful. If you can't answer that in a heartbeat, you need to go back and really think about why you're doing everything because until you can do that, you won't get over that hurdle because you'll find every reason not to do something. If 'your why' isn't strong enough, you won't be motivated to get over the crappy days, the dark mornings, and the rainy, cold winter and do what you set out to achieve. For me, that is the fundamental foundation for everything within high performance and sales and what we do because, without that, you will just fall apart.

Simon: Yes, you must identify what success means for you. It could be a loving family; it could be a marriage; it could be relationships; it could be money. Whatever goals you have in your life, always ask if your behaviour reflects those goals. If the answer is yes, crack on; good job, and keep going. You're on the right track! If the answer is no, you can only do two things. The first thing is to downgrade the results you want. The second thing you can do is change your behaviour. But the problem is most people want the same best possible results but don't want to change their behaviour. People want to lose weight, but they're eating cream cakes. So, make sure your behaviour is aligned with the results you want.

Steve: Lots of changes, lots of things impacting over the last couple of years with COVID and changes in working habits and things. What do you see as the biggest challenges we face due to the changes?

The biggest challenges we face.

Thinking differently. Post-pandemic, every day is a school day; you learn something new each time. It's also frustrating because it doesn't have stability, but as long as we're all working effectively to ensure we achieve something, then we're okay. My view on hybrid working from home is to choose whatever's right for the organisation and the individuals, although some research has said that, on average, workers are 30% less productive working from home than when they're in the office with each other. Especially in the sales environment; it's a vibrant environment, you're bouncing off each other, perhaps with the old fashioned 'ringing the bell', standing up on the phone, and all those great things. If you're working from home, however, it's difficult to feel the same excitement. We've got to open our minds to the opportunity for change, progression and sustainability.

One Single Piece of Advice

Make sure your behaviour is aligned with the results you want. Ensure that what you're currently doing, or what you plan to do, is aligned with what you say you want to achieve in any aspect of life. Then do everything you've got to do to keep doing it. I sometimes wear T-shirts with slogans on them just to be provocative. Some of the quotes are;

"Nothing is good or bad, but thinking makes it so."

Another is:

"Sure, it is. What we do about it?"

My favourite is this one, "Do it or don't do it, just don't whinge about it."

If you want to be successful in whatever aspect of your life, what are you doing about it? So many things can knock you off your track, so don't be one of those people telling yourself you can't do it.

Also, one of the things we say in our management program is we can't motivate people. People are self-motivated. We as managers have to create the right conditions which enable people to perform tasks willingly and to the best of their ability.

Simon Thorpe's Key Takeaways

* Simon emphasises that mindset is the fundamental trait that separates high performers from anyone else.
* Resilience and mental toughness are also key factors in high performance.
* To achieve high performance, individuals must anticipate potential obstacles and be prepared to deal with them.
* What-if thinking can help individuals be prepared for any eventuality.
* Doing something that others aren't doing can help individuals be the best in their field.
* Coping with stress can be problem-focused or emotion-focused.
* It's important to focus on what you can fix and deal with emotions in a positive way when faced with a situation that cannot be changed.
* Don't share your goals with too many people, as external validation may make you lose motivation.
* Ask close people to check in with you once a month to create a commitment to achieve your goals.

- Have the commitment to keep moving forward and do what you say you're going to do.
- Failure is part of resilience and an opportunity to learn and get better.
- Spend a few minutes at the end of each day to reflect on what you achieved and how to improve the next day.
- Adopt a growth mindset, and don't limit yourself based on past failures or weaknesses.
- Be aware of the negativity bias and pay attention to what's going on in your brain.

Contact Simon

Just put my name into LinkedIn. I love to chat and put a few provocative posts out there as good fun. I don't mind having an argument, a discussion, or a debate.

Email : s.thorpe@expressionspartnership.com
Twitter : @expressions2003

Simon's Q&A

What's your version of success?

Making a positive and sustainable difference to people and performance in any aspect of life.

Top three books to read or listen to?

The 7 Habits of Highly Effective People – Stephen Covey
Black Box Thinking – Matthew Syed
The Boy, the Mole, The Fox and the Horse – Charlie Mackesy

What's your favourite quote?

Without wishing to be arrogant, it's one of my own quotes, which is "Do it or Don't Do it, Just Don't Whinge about it"!

What advice would you give your younger self?

What other people think about you is none of your business. Don't let them affect you because you are accountable for your feelings, beliefs, and actions.

What is the best investment you have made, and why?

Investment in time studying and learning to understand why people behave the way they do. I have been so privileged to meet and discuss these subjects with some great minds.

What's your go-to productivity trick?

It's a simple sticker we give out at our Management Academy, and I use it myself. It has a simple question – What's the BEST use of my time Right Now? It sharpens the mind and allows me to pause and check my compass instead of my clock.

If you could write a book about your life, what would the title be and why?

'If you're happy and you know it, tell your face.'

What's one thing you're learning now, and why is it important?

You cannot help those who do not want to help themselves. It's not my job to change the world, but I will do all I can to play my part. Unfortunately, some people expect everyone else to do it for them. Personal accountability is essential for sustainable improvement.

Who would you choose if you could trade places with anyone for a day?

My wife, so I could properly understand what it's like to live with me and what I could do to learn from this experience and improve. Just don't tell her that, though, eh?

CHAPTER ELEVEN

Mike Whatman

(High Performance / Leadership)

About Mike

Mike has worked in the recruitment industry for nearly 12 years, starting as a trainee consultant at a life sciences executive search firm before working his way up the ladder to principal consultant, top billing status, and up to team leader of million-pound teams. As part of the expansion of the business at the time, Mike was tasked with building a fit-for-purpose learning and development function to support the growth of the business into the US, Asia, Pacific and Europe, with new starters all the way up to sales managers across the globe, in order to maximise the potential of all involved playing a major role in the rapid growth of the business. Outside of work, Mike is a professional rugby coach, having learnt his trade at Leicester Tigers with the academy before becoming the youngest director of rugby within the National League setup. He has also coached elite rowing and football and brings with him a wealth of experience from the tried and tested people and cultural development strategies within elite sports. Now running a leadership consultancy business called Mike Whatman Consulting that works specifically within the recruitment industry with small to medium-sized businesses who are looking to scale by investing in their leadership teams to create high-performance cultures and develop winning mindsets. This individual has worked with over 2000 recruitment leaders worldwide over the past few years.

In Mike's own words:

I have very broad experience, and I've been lucky that by a young age, to have experienced a huge amount of different high-performance environments. My approach to leadership and people development combines psychology, neuroscience, and business acumen from doing the job for so long as well. I specialise in empowering individuals to accomplish what may have seemed unattainable to them in the past, offering a unique approach that distinguishes itself from traditional management training programmes. I think people find it interesting to link sports, neuroscience and psychology to see how they can learn, maximise their potential, and achieve things they didn't think possible.

Do sport and recruitment correlate?

Steve: *You've worked in sport at an elite level. Do you think the intensity, the competition, and the level of expectancy from that level of sport correlate to the competitive environment of business and recruitment?*

Mike: Yeah, for sure, but there are some things that don't correlate. In professional sports, you're training 95% of the time and playing 5%. Whereas in recruitment, you're doing your job 95% of the time, and training for maybe 5% of the time, so there are some huge disparities there. To be successful in both, there's a huge amount that can be learnt because those who are top performers, irrelevant of their field, whether it be rugby or recruitment, are the ones that are continually getting better, the ones that are continually looking to learn, and focus on the process, and focus on their performance rather than the outcomes. Obviously, some people can be very outcome-focused and cut corners to get there. In sport, that might be by taking something that's illegal so they can run 100 metres faster, or in recruitment, it's ignoring people's exclusivity and sending CVs. To actually find consistent success, there are many parallels that you can pull across by consistency and performance, focusing on their processes rather than the outcomes, constantly learning and striving to try and get better. These are the crossover parallels where the top performers in each field share those traits.

There is a huge amount that we can take from the world of elite sport that can actually help us improve our efficiency and what we're doing as recruiters and recruitment leaders and make us more profitable without having to do a huge amount of work behind it. Combining the two has really helped me in my career.

Creating Habits

Steve: *My recruitment career over the last 18 years has championed process and organised systems. I love stats – anything that combines numbers and strategy. That's what has set me apart from pretty much all of my competition in recruitment, which is a largely outgoing, loudest person in the room type of environment. You succinctly put within your answer there the fact that systems and process, whether it be sport or business, helps you to see the incremental 1% gains along the way and how they are far more powerful in the long run.*

Mike: We talk about processes, but really, you're creating habits, and that's the key. You can call them systems, processes, and habits, but it's about identifying the behaviours and activities that you're doing a lot of – because success leaves clues when things are going well. So, when things are going well, what are you doing, and what kind of activity levels are you at? What kind of activities are you doing? Successful teams in sport or business have identified those winning behaviours, and to be successful, they implement those behaviours. Everyone in that team knows that, and that then becomes their system, their processes and their habit. For example, the Barcelona football team under Pep Guardiola went through a huge period of time where they were unbeatable. There were two key behaviours that they knew if they did every game, they would win.

1. As soon as the team lost possession of the ball, every player on the pitch would hound the ball for the next five seconds. They understood that the moment you gain possession is when you're most likely to lose it because you're not in the right setup. Based on their experience, they knew that by hounding the ball, there was a greater chance of winning it back. It was ingrained in every player to know exactly what to do as soon as they lost the ball.

2. They would win if they had more than 65% to 70% possession in a game. So, they focused on keeping the ball, keeping possession and tiring people out.

They knew they were more likely to win if they consistently performed these two systems in every game. In business, it's finding out your version of hounding them or finding out your version of 70% possession. What does that look like for you, your business, your team, and your company? You must ensure everyone's on the same page, knows what it takes, and is clear on their role. It gives you more time because no one's asking me questions, but all are pulling in the same direction that we know generates success. That's an unstoppable force.

Process

Steve: *I hadn't heard that story before, and I'm an avid football fan! That analogy brings us back to the ability to deliver on the deliverables or control the controllable. You hear it bandied about quite a lot in recruitment at the moment. You mentioned earlier that recruiters often would focus on the end fee or their end productivity regarding* how many placements they have made this month. What's the end fee value once they have hit the target? The problem is that you're focusing on the end result, not how you get there. When I'm talking to recruiters quite often, I will say, "You need to focus on the front end, understand how to get to where you need to be and work backwards. You need to know how many CVs to get out, how many interviews you need to be arranging, and how many conversations you need to have to get to that point. The fees will take care of themselves if you do enough upfront work.

Mike: If you focus on the process and you focus on the activity, the results look after themselves. If you're doing the right activity, that's the key, so you must take the time to understand what is the right activity. Once you're doing that, don't worry about the outcomes because they will look after themselves. However, if you just focus on outcomes, you'll only think it's a success if you hit that outcome. If you don't hit it, that's a failure. We have a binary idea of hitting a target, and if you miss your target a few times, you are constantly reinforcing the idea and belief system that you're failing, which creates self-limiting self-belief and self-doubt. That increases stress on the body, which isn't healthy. Whereas if you focus on the process and let the outcomes look after themselves, you're removing that stress input. Try not to simply focus on the output, as it's also healthier for your body.

Growth Mindset

Steve: In your bio, we discussed having a growth mindset and practising that. It's something that I've had to get used to, and I don't know whether it's a typical British thing, like when people say, "How are you doing?".

"Oh, I'm not too bad." This is how we often respond.

But what that does is focus on the fact that you're not as bad as you could be. In its simplest form, having a growth mindset does not necessarily come naturally.

Mike: The cool thing about the growth mindset is that it can be developed. You may think you have a fixed mindset around certain things, but with the right action and attitude, a growth mindset can be developed and made better just by delivering the right actions. It's about changing the narrative in your head. Rather than thinking, "I'm not going to hit that target because the markets slow" (which is a definitive statement point), instead change it to a 'what if?' question.

"What if I just get one client who's all of a sudden hiring? The market doesn't need to be really busy. If I can just get one client who's hiring two people, I can hit my target."

It's about changing the conversations you have inside your head, working on them and not seeing things as finite. Also, look back from when you started to where you are now and appreciate the growth. Take the time for yourself, and change the conversations you're having. Rather than direct statements, ask them 'what if?' questions and start developing a growth mindset.

Challenges are outside your comfort zone, and it's where growth happens. Your brain has potential in terms of the talent you've developed and the skills you've harnessed over time. And the optimal level of difficulty to help your brain develop is 4% harder than your ability. The point is that if you stretch yourself just enough, you can develop yourself, and that's the optimal way to keep improving. Of course, you can't learn nuclear physics from scratch right now for a university test tomorrow because that's just too difficult. But equally, if it's too easy, your brain doesn't develop, stretch, or form neuroplasticity.

Negativity Bias

We are negatively biased. The brain is wired to protect us, so we can be constantly aware of threats. That's why we systemise everything. Part of the work I do with leaders is about giving feedback. Most people find giving negative or developmental feedback so much easier than giving positive feedback. Positive feedback sounds forced, contrived, or fake, whereas negative feedback is easier for us. If we don't understand something, we're more likely to say "no", which is why we do Business Development work. If the client doesn't understand why you're calling or what your value is, they're more likely to say, "No, thank you, we're not interested". Whereas if your value is clearer, the reason for your call is clearer, and they understand, they're more likely to engage, answer questions and give you some time.

Characteristics of high-level performers

Steve: *We were talking about developing and creating high-performance cultures and a winning mindset. What would you say, from a recruitment perspective, when you have run-of-the-mill recruiters that are good at what they do, they do a decent return, they hit their targets, yet they go unnoticed because they just do what they are expected to do? And then you've got these people that come in, let's call them 'Mavericks' that fly through anything, with fees and placements happening all over the place. What is the difference between your average level of performance and that elite level of high performance? What are the character traits?*

Mike: High performance is about consistently delivering to the best of your ability at that time. It's about controlling the controllable. One of the really cool things about working in recruitment is that we're working with people, and we get to talk, learn from people and have interesting conversations. But then one of the biggest challenges of working in recruitment is that we're working with people, and they can constantly change their minds. They can make behavioural decisions based on the mood of their cat that day! Some things we can't control, and for me, high performance in recruitment is about consistently delivering to the best of your ability at that time. It is also the ability to understand what it takes, from an activity perspective, what it is to be successful. What are your winning behaviours? Understand and have clarity on what your winning behaviours are. Consistency and performance are about limiting the gap between good days and bad days because everyone knows if you've worked in recruitment for more than 45 minutes, it's a peak and trough nature. You will always see it in any recruitment business. Elite performers have the ability to limit the difference between a good and a bad day because that prevents the gap size between the peak and the trough. When they're in a big trough, you've got a long way to go to get back to a peak again. Whereas if the difference is minimal, you're constantly projecting and on a good trajectory of consistent growth.

If you've got contract runners, they're constantly building; if you've got perm fees, it's constantly building. When there is a massive discrepancy between good and bad contract runners, the good runners can get too high and fall off a cliff. Then you have to work extra hard to get them back to where they were, only for them to fall off a cliff again. Those performers will constantly bill £150,000 every year, right, whereas the guys and girls who elicit that consistency and limit the difference between good and bad will go from £150,000 the next year to £200,000 the next £500,000 and continue to accelerate. In recruitment, the foundation for high performance is, firstly, consistently doing your best at that time and understanding what behaviours and activities are needed to be successful. Then you must limit the gap between good and bad because that enables you to consistently grow, rather than having to constantly fight against the tide when you have a bad plan. If you can nail those three things, you're on your way to making some really good revenue for both the business and yourself.

How to keep a winning mindset?

It's about having the systems and processes to know that you've done your best. You can then think, "I've done everything that I can do. I've asked every question. I've delivered, and I prepared them for the interview properly. I prepared the client as well as I could."

There's a lot to be said about self-confidence and success in recruitment, but equally, if you have the ability at the end of each day to look in the mirror and ask, "Did I try my hardest to do everything I could do today?" If you can look in the mirror and say "yes" to that, then you can have the confidence to not win every deal.

I remember my second hiring process; a lady turned down the role the day before she was meant to start after completing her four-week notice. She called me up and said, "I'm not going to be able to take the role because I haven't been able to find anyone to look after my pedigree cat and feed them lunch."

I didn't even know pedigree cats existed! It was a Friday afternoon, and we went out for drinks afterwards, as you did back in 2011. I was furious at this cat and furious at the lady, and I couldn't figure out why she hadn't told me. But then, if I think about it, it's my fault. I didn't ask her if there was anything that would prevent her from accepting the contract. I should have asked, "Is there anything outside of work that would prevent you from being able to travel there every day?"

We all try to blame externally, but actually, if I do that mirror thing and ask, "Did I do everything?" in that case, the answer is no – I didn't ask that question. What I learnt from that situation, moving forward, is that I asked everyone if they had a cat for every process for the next however many years! "What cat have you got? Is it going to catch me out?"

But on a serious note, that was my second week in recruitment, and I remember thinking it was ridiculous, but it taught me a great lesson.

Failure

Steve: *In any career path, whether that be in sport or in business, there are always failures along the way, which can be turning points that change your directional path. What would you say has been the biggest failure, and what was the end result?*

Mike: My life has always been around high-performance environments. Whether it be elite rugby or executive search in business, it's about who's got the biggest watch? Who makes the most money? Who's got the biggest house? And then you go to the Rugby Club, and it's about who lifts the most and who hits the hardest. When I was a 22-year old kid I saw people billing half a million quid and then off to Dubai every three weeks, with the Porsche in the carpark, and I wanted it. So, rather than focusing on the process and how they got there by being successful, putting in the hours, and understanding their market, I just created a character to fit in. I ended up living my life to impress other people. I was getting success also, which was fuelling the fire. It meant that I created a persona who was not a great person – not the kind of person you want your daughter to bring home.

I realised I was living to impress others. I still thought being the loudest in the room and being the richest of my friends, and the most successful was what the role required. About three years ago, I was very unwell and spent a lot of time in the hospital and had two surgeries to keep me alive. On the second time that I was being taken down to the operating theatre, I heard the surgeon say to my wife, "He might not come back up from this". All of a sudden, it dawned on me that the life I'd been living didn't matter. All this material stuff. Who cares? Why have I been living a life for somebody else? I've wasted so much time. I could have been creating memories doing stuff for me and focusing on myself and what's important to me, like family and friends and personal development and giving back. That was my biggest failure – running somebody else's race. I was trying to impress others and act in a way that I thought the recruitment world needed. I thought it was what was needed to be respected. But it's not that at all.

My biggest learning now is 'run your own race'. You don't need to impress anyone because you can become exhausted running somebody else's race. Focus on yourself. Focus on what's important to you because true wealth is memories. It was my daughter's first birthday the other day, and I spent the entire day creating memories, taking photos, and playing in the garden because that's what's important – that's what true wealth is. And that's what you're going to be remembered for, the legacy that you leave behind, not the cars or watches or a number of contractors. My biggest failing was thinking that in order to be successful in recruitment, I had to be somebody that I wasn't.

Influential People

Steve: *I'm a firm advocate that if you have mentors, coaches and positive people around you, it will elevate you and get you to where you want to go. Who would you say have been the most influential people to you?*

Mike: My granddad. He instilled in me how important manners are in life; he said, "Manners will get you everywhere". He was a hugely successful businessman and left school when he was 12, with no qualifications, and worked in a sausage factory for a while, and then ended up working on a building site. He ended up owning the building company and building most of the South East of England. He was very successful and retired by the age of 50. Secondly, he taught me work ethics and that nothing is ever given. You must work hard and put the effort in if you want to be a success. The third thing that he taught me is to always ask people questions. Whenever you meet someone, ask them a question. Always show an interest because you never know who you're going to meet and what you're going to learn from them. Never judge someone until you know their story. I love talking to new people.

The other person I admire is Tiger Woods, from a sporting perspective. I understand he has had his misdemeanours, and that's not the part of him that I admire and aspire to. I admire and aspire to his ability to rewrite how golf can be played and how it can be done. I had the privilege of meeting him when I was younger, and while they say "never meet your heroes", he was an absolute gentleman and gave me all the time in the world. He let me ask loads of questions, signed my hat and was an absolute gentleman. A couple of years ago, he had back injuries and knee injuries, and he was told he would probably never play golf again, but through hard work, determination and endeavour, he managed to bring himself back around, recovered, and rehabbed. From a sporting perspective, he's had a huge influence on me in terms of seeing what's in front of me, and I won't be afraid to try something different. Equally, never be told no; if you want something enough, you can return to the top of the mountain.

The other two people that have probably had the biggest impact are my wife and my little girl; everything's for them.

One piece of advice

Run your own race. Understand what's important to you, have clarity on what you want to achieve, understand how you're going to get there and then just focus on your lane. Don't worry about what the person next to you is doing. Don't worry about next week or next month; just focus on the here and now, and be present in what you're doing. Focus on what's important to you. Run your own race.

I promise you if you increase your clarity in where you're trying to get to and you increase the clarity on how you're going to get there, you will notice an improvement because you're being channelled in the right direction. Rather than being over here, over there, and spreading yourself too thin, if you have that clarity, you understand where you're going and how to get there.

In summary

- Creating habits is crucial for success in business and sport, as it allows for consistent performance.
- Successful teams identify winning behaviours, which become their processes and habits.
- In business, finding out what works and consistently performing those actions leads to success.
- Focusing on the front end, understanding how to get there, and developing processes is more powerful in the long run than solely focusing on the end result.
- Consistently deliver to the best of your ability and control the controllable.
- Limit the gap between good and bad days to achieve consistency in growth.
- Have self-confidence and be prepared not to win every deal.
- Learn from failures and use them as turning points.
- Ask yourself if you have done everything possible at the end of each day.
- Build self-confidence and success by knowing that you have done your best.
- Take responsibility for your mistakes and learn from them.
- Don't blame external factors.

Contact Mike

Find me on LinkedIn as Michael Whatman – that's the best place to find me. Follow me for content as well to keep getting stuff to help you along the way.

https://mikewhatmanconsulting.co.uk/

Mike's Q&A

What's your version of success?

Maximising your potential against the opportunity that you have in front of you

Top three books to read or listen to?

The Coaching Habit – Michael Bungay Stanier
Hooked – Nir Eyal
Thinking Fast and Slow – Daniel Kahnemann

What's your favourite quote?

Work hard in silence; let your success be your noise
– Frank Ocean.

What advice would you give your younger self?

Be who you are rather than the person you think that you need to be.

What is the best investment you have made, and why?

Investing in good people around me so that I am surrounded by people who push me and inspire me.

What's your go-to productivity trick?

Chunking – break the big goal down into shorter time-based objectives.

If you could write a book about your life, what would the title be and why?

I did; it was called Run your own race. I wrote it because I spent so much of my life trying to live up to a character. I was measuring my success based on other people, rather than staying true to myself and creating my own version of success.

What's one thing you're learning now, and why is it important?

Be present; life is precious, and every moment you waste, you can't get back. Don't worry about things you can't control, and just enjoy the now.

Who would you choose if you could trade places with anyone for a day?

My two-year-old. To find so much joy in the simplest of things. Not have any idea about the pressures of growing up. Twelve hours of sleep every day and then 12 hours of playing and creating memories without a care in the world.

CHAPTER TWELVE

Jeremy Snell

(Recruitment)

About Jeremy

Jeremy has trained over 9000 recruiters across 18 different countries. He is a recruitment trainer on a mission to help recruiters win more clients, be more productive, drive trackable returns on investments, and have more fun along the way.

In Jeremy's own words:

Jeremy: I was at Hays Recruitment for eight years, and it was a great stomping ground. Anyone there today may not recognise the Hays that I used to work at. I worked there when they had just bought a business called 'Accountancy Personnel'. I was part of the business straight after the acquisition and learnt a lot while working there.

There was a cold call boot camp. You were sat in this boiler room making 100 cold calls a day, and if that didn't grind it out of you, then you got promoted to go into the office.

Steve: *Yes, that's right! I remember that. Hays created me into the recruiter that I am today in terms of structure, process, procedure, and having a plan. You also talk a lot about habits and behaviour, so how do you think habits frame whether you're an average recruiter or a successful recruiter?*

Habits

Jeremy: Every single recruiter has habits, some of which they've deliberately installed out of choice, and some have been installed by accident. There's a myth that if we practice really hard, we'll get good at something, yet that isn't true. Because when we practice something really hard, we simply make it permanent. Do we choose what we want to practice? Do we ask, "What do I want my future behaviours and habits to be?". It's important to know because we can accidentally practice something so much that it becomes a permanent habit that then becomes difficult to unpick. Experienced recruiters may unintentionally fall into habitual patterns, which poses a challenge for them. It becomes difficult to break free from these habits because they are often unaware of the ingrained behaviours that have developed through their practises.

Steve: *Completely. I'm a habitual person, and I have structure in everything I do. That said, over the 18 years of recruiting, the habits I made when I was initially trained as a recruiter are different from those I have now. Even as a seasoned recruiter, you can become a little stale and forget those great things that worked years ago.*

Jeremy: Yes, you can describe being structured as a habit, but some people are unstructured, and that's their habit; they are habitually disorganised, and they're habitually unstructured in what they do. You must start thinking about what you want your future habits to be, and once you introduce the idea of deciding what your future habits will be, that becomes your practice routine. When you practice doing that every day from today, it becomes permanent, and then you arrive at that point in the future where it's become a habit. I'm not sure enough people in recruitment are thinking about the habits they want at the end of this month or next year. Maybe they are not asking how close they are to being inconsistent. We become inconsistent halfway between not doing it and making it a habit. So, if we can measure being inconsistent this month and then measure incremental increases in consistency over the course of the next six weeks, then we should arrive at a point where we are consistently consistent, and the inconsistency has stopped.

Reframing

Steve: *As humans, we shield ourselves with self-limiting beliefs that try to protect the fear of failure or rejection. How do you deal with that?*

Jeremy: I've helped some people deal with not being very good at cold calls by saying that we will stop doing that forever and do a new type of call called 'coaching calls'. In a coaching call, we phone some businesses and coach them on how to recruit better. So, we need to ask them good questions about how they currently recruit, understand their challenges, and what they aspire to achieve in terms of results. Then we advise them on how they could do that, which might involve working with us. So, I say, "Let's just do 20 coaching calls this week," Suddenly, people with a cold call phobia are into it because they have reframed.

The phrase 'cold call' will create a chemical release in somebody's body, let's say adrenaline, which thinks, "We're going to have an argument here." or "I'm just going to run and hide." "I'm going to go back to resourcing that job that I was looking at yesterday because that's my comfort zone." If you think about 'cold calls', you might get cortisol in your body, which is a stress chemical and start to get really anxious. But when you reframe it, no chemical response is associated with that trigger. If you do coaching calls instead, you might start to feel a bit excited, maybe with a bit of serotonin and some oxytocin going. Then, you wonder where all these positive feelings have been all of your life.

Successful Behaviour

Steve: *How do you ensure that you're behaving well, have the right mindset and act in a certain way to stimulate the best results?*

Jeremy: Successful behaviour is normally linked to a good process and structure. When you've got process and structure, and you can follow that consistently then you're able to say this is my proven placement process ABCDEFG+ all the way through to completion. Now that you've got that mapped out, and you know what each of those stages are, you can now focus on how you do it rather than thinking, 'Where am I going next with this?' When you can start to think about 'how do I now deliver that particular component?' That's the behaviour bit. 'How do I need to behave at this moment to be able to ensure that I do that task to the best of my ability without the mapped-out process, proven placement process, proven sales process, or proven structure for a client meeting? Well, in that case, you end up winging it, which many recruiters do because they've learnt that habit. They rely on this thing called 'flair'. Flair is far more linked to the mood they are in, and thus when you start to put flair above following a robust process, you will really start to see a change in pace.

Behavioural Change

Behavioural change comes by asking, "What could I have done earlier in the process to prevent a sticky client situation? What could I have done earlier in the process to recognise that the client was behaving differently than they told me that they were going to?" That requires some focus, some discipline and a willingness to accept that everything is your fault. When everything is your fault, you can look at the situation differently and decide "where could I have changed?" If you then go back to that behaviour moment and think "that's what I can do differently", that's really powerful. Twice as powerful when you look at what succeeded and say "why was that my fault?" When you do an autopsy on success, you get better quicker than when you perform an autopsy on failure.

If you manage a team of people on boardroom Friday, you say, "We're going to go through the week". Everyone's expecting to do an autopsy of failure, not, "You did really well; you did 25 calls and got nine jobs on. Let's learn what happened in those 25 calls that created nine jobs." Rather than picking the bones out of the job that fell over, instead, say, "We filled six jobs this week. Let's get them all up on the board, and see what they share in common, and do more things that look like that."

My daughter is home-schooling, and she had a maths homework thing. She submitted it. "How'd you get on with your maths?" I said.

"I've got three wrong." She said.

"How many did you get correct?" I said

"25"

"So why are we talking about the three wrong?" I said.

"Well, they're the ones with the red crosses."

"Well, let's enjoy the 25 ticks for a moment before we think about the crosses."

If you manage a team, I feel it's part of our responsibility to fix that in people because people feel more empowered when they recognise what they can do well. Then we help people to lean into their strengths. When you lean into a strength, you are more motivated to do that thing, which drives behaviour. How we think drives how we feel, and how we feel drives how we act. So, if we want to see people acting in a certain way, including ourselves, we've got to change how we think, which will change how we feel about the activity. If we start to change how we feel about the activity, we can start to think, "I've got this. I know what worked."

Objection Handling

Strangely, one of the most common questions I ask recruiters and businesses about training requests is objection handling and how to deal with it. Most of the time, I say, "Well, you need to stop bringing it up!" So, lesson one in objection handling is to stop bringing it up.

Dear reader, regarding writing emails, if the following is you, please stop doing it.

'Dear Bob,

I hope you're well in these unprecedented and dangerous times when many people are currently dying. I thought I'd brighten your day by sharing three positive things that are going on within the industry at the moment.'

Don't do it; it's naval gazing.

Writing an email demands more thought than a conversation. Conversations happen synchronously, allowing thoughts to flow naturally, while condensing ideas into a brief email requires more thought than a five-minute conversation.

Only 23% of emails in a business-to-business environment in the UK get opened, so there is a whopping 77% chance your email isn't going to get opened. We think to ourselves, "I emailed them yesterday, so they're clearly not interested" Or rather, "I know that I emailed them, and I'm sure they opened it and immediately decided it is a no, and so calling them would be like crazy right?" Call them; it's likely the email wasn't opened.

Inspiration

Steve: *You've had 25 years in recruitment now. Who are the people that have inspired you and had an impact on where you are now?*

Jeremy: If I go right back to the beginning, the person who inspired me the most was a guy called Steven Finkel, who wrote a book and did some videos, and then came to the company that I worked at to deliver training. He spoke in the same flavour as I thought, and it clicked. I was just lucky to be in the right place at the right time and that he turned out to be that person.

Then there are a couple of people I'm not going to name who inspired me for all the wrong reasons because they taught me everything that I didn't want to be. There have been some managers where you sit there and think, "When I'm a manager, I'm not going to be you."

Then, there is James Altucher, who wrote a book called 'Choose Yourself', which is about getting comfortable with who you are as a person, because until you accept who you are, it's going to be very difficult to get other people to accept who you are. He writes great blogs that revolve around investment, money and business. I like his thoughts and how he sees things, and he is the epitome of whatever the advice is in the world; he recommends doing the opposite.

I feel that I'm in the same place. If this is what everyone's telling recruiters to do, that's where the pack is going. If we can see what's happening in recruitment, then do the opposite.

Key traits of high-performers

Steve: *Looking at your journey through recruitment, you've engaged, trained, mentored, and coached a huge amount of individuals across cultural differences, countries, and destinations. What characteristics do you find in a person who consistently excels and drives high performance?*

Jeremy: One high-performing trait is consistent self-awareness, making you mindful of how you're impacting other people. Whether that's getting on the phone to talk to a candidate about a job and getting too fixated on selling the job rather than doing the right assessment, think, "Have I fallen in love with some buzzwords on a CV? And therefore, I'm blind to everything else. How am I dealing with this human being rather than chasing a CV?" It's the same with more senior consultants; they're projecting behavioural leadership to others around them. They might be projecting behaviours that others will emulate that might not be best for everybody.

Another high-performing trait is putting energy into stuff. If you're going to do something, do it properly and do it with energy. When you approach a task with energy, it helps establish a cadence that adds a sense of urgency, ensuring its completion. Afterwards, it's essential to transition to other tasks, as lingering on it unnecessarily will only prolong the process. You have more energy when doing something in a short timeframe.

The last one is courage. There is a guy in London I did some training with and still talk to. Before he went into recruitment, he'd done tenure service in para one (training for the SAS) tours of Afghanistan, and Iraq. He'd been shot in the head, jumped out of planes, and failed SAS selection twice. After failing selection, he got into recruitment, recruiting contractors. On his first day, when I was training him in sales, he said to me, "Jeremy, I've never been this scared in my life. You're asking me to do my first ever cold call, and I'm more scared doing this than I was running at people with a gun in my hand being shot at."

That's an example of being asked to do something outside of your comfort zone. He essentially said, "Shoot at me if you want, but I'm terrified to pick up the phone". There are people courageous enough to go into a burning building to rescue a kitten or run up a hill towards an enemy who is firing at them with RPGs. Our definition of courage in recruitment is, "Phone that bloke!"

Courage is required in so many little doses in this job, like the moment when somebody says. "I'm not looking for a job". We are always presented with two paths: the path of least resistance and the path of maximum reward. It is the person who is courageous enough when no one is watching who picks the path of maximum reward. Who is willing to challenge, willing to ask a question, willing to stand by the strength of their convictions and say, "No, it's 25%!" and not go off to their manager to say, "I've got a really good deal. They'll give it to us exclusively, as long as it's 15%."

The courage moment wasn't negotiating with your manager but with the other person. All these situations mean courage must be turned on 25 times daily. And as long as you can turn on courage more than 50% of the time, you'll make headway. If you keep taking the path of least resistance and no one returns your voicemails, no one wants to talk to you, and no one is willing to pay you 18% because everyone else is paying 10%, it's the 'courage' part that's missing because, at that moment, you can either take the path of least resistance or the path of most reward.

I'd take standing for the 25% rather than having a grenade thrown at me. I'll take talking to a candidate about the merits of considering looking at a new job rather than having to run into a petrol station that's on fire and get paid more! I get paid more for being courageous at home; I just need to be courageous at home more frequently.

How to find Jeremy

Find me on LinkedIn, and send me a message. You can find me on my website, which is talentbuilder.co.uk. You can find my mobile number on my LinkedIn profile, and you can call me without an appointment. And as long as I answer it, we could start with "hello". Or you could drop me an email, and I would quite happily respond to 23% of the emails I receive.

Key Takeaways

- Habits are important in recruitment, and recruiters should deliberately choose the habits they want to have in the future.
- Recruiters must be aware that they can accidentally practice bad habits, which can be difficult to unpick.
- Reframing can be useful for dealing with self-limiting beliefs and fear of failure or rejection.
- Successful behaviour is usually linked to having a good process and structure, and recruiters should focus on how they deliver each component of the process to ensure the best results.

Objection Handling:

- Avoid bringing up objections unnecessarily during a conversation.
- Avoid hammering out hundreds of emails and prefer synchronous, engaging conversations.
- If an email goes unanswered, consider calling the recipient, as it's likely that the email wasn't opened.

Inspiration:

- Seek inspiration from people who speak in a way that resonates with you.
- Learn from people who demonstrate what you don't want to be.
- Accept yourself to gain acceptance from others.

Key traits of high-performers:

- Consistent self-awareness to be mindful of how you're impacting other people.
- Putting energy into things and doing them with urgency.
- Courage to step outside of your comfort zone, such as picking up the phone to call someone.

Contact Jeremy

Email – jeremy@rookie2recruiter.com
Website – https://rookie2recruiter.com/
Socials – https://www.linkedin.com/in/recruitmentsalestraining/

Jeremy's Q&A

What's your version of success?

A big question to answer and one where the real answer is often very personal. To answer this, I had to start by confirming to myself what it isn't (for me). It's not material. It can't be bought. It's less of a goal and more of a discipline. To me, true success is happiness – being happy with who I am, what I do and the satisfaction I get from life. I've carried a piece of paper in my wallet with my dedication list on it. I look at it daily to help me stay focused on being the best version of myself (happy) I can be.

Top three books to read or listen to?

Choose Yourself – James Altucher
Eating the Big Fish – Adam Morgan
Eat Their Lunch – Anthony Iannarino

Funny that two out of three are about eating. Especially as on my dedication list is "Hara Hachi Bu", which is Japanese for "eat until 80% full."

What's your favourite quote?

"No one is you, and that is your power" – Dave Grohl

What advice would you give your younger self?

Focus on what you really want from life and spend less time worrying about what other people think. Some of the decisions you're going to make, other people will tell you you're making a mistake. When you get older, you'll realise that you did the right thing – even if they were right. It's all going to work out fine in the end.

What is the best investment you have made, and why?

I spent £2.47 on a pack of A5 record cards and £3.79 on a photo album to put them in when I started in recruitment. They became my objection handling playbook. They had all my scripts and rebuttals on them that gave me the real-time support to build a career in recruitment as a consistent biller. Less than £7.00 was spent to underwrite my 25+ year career in recruitment.

What's your go-to productivity trick?

Working hard. It's not a trick, so it doesn't appeal to everyone. Everyone craves a hack that plays to the desire to achieve more from doing less. My goal is to be the hardest-working person in the metaphorical room.

If you could write a book about your life, what would the title be and why?

Lessons in luck. I reflect back on life and can see that I've had a habit of being in the right place at the right time. That's an element of luck that's outside of my control. I seem to have fallen on my feet into the things that I've done and then used energy to work hard at them. I fell into being a wine taster. I then fell into working in a bucking bronco bar in Ibiza, then falling into recruitment and then falling into L&D before falling into starting my business. Luck got me to each of those points.

What's one thing you're learning now, and why is it important?

I'm finally committed to a dedicated regime to play the guitar to a good standard. I've been a casual learner for a long time and realised how little I've improved, so I'm now being far more purposeful with my practice. I love music, and it's a big part of my life, so being able to play the tunes I love is rewarding.

Who would you choose if you could trade places with anyone for a day?

Eddie Vedder – lead singer from Pearl Jam. I want to know what it feels like to have 100,000 people singing back at me. If I could pick the song, it would HAVE to be Jeremy.

Conclusion

In Steve's own words:

As we come to the end of The Guestlist, I want to thank you, the reader, for embarking on this journey with me. I hope that the insights and knowledge shared by our guests have been valuable to you and that you have been challenged to broaden your horizons and explore new perspectives.

One of the most common themes across all chapters of this book is the importance of mindset. Time and time again, our guests emphasise that a positive attitude adjustment can transform everything for the better. They have learnt that the right mentality is key to overcoming obstacles, achieving goals, and ultimately, finding success. In fact, every single person I interviewed for this book has never given up, and that kind of resilience can only come from having a strong and positive mind. All the guests have realised the power of a positive attitude adjustment and the illusion of failure.

I sincerely hope that the tales and lessons in this book have motivated you and that you are now prepared to take action and continue to achieve extraordinary success in your field.

If you want to learn more about any of the guests or their businesses, please do not hesitate to get in touch with them or me. I would love to hear your feedback and how this book has impacted your life.

Once again, thank you for reading The Guestlist. I wish you all the best on your journey, and may you continue to expand your knowledge, challenge your assumptions, and gain fresh insights that can transform your career and life.

Until next time, good luck.

Steve Guest

Contact Steve

steve@sguest.co.uk
https://www.linkedin.com/in/steveguest1/

The End.

→ Follow people that inspire me

→ 10 year plan

→ Bus. where are we going & why?

→ Read! ~~1 book a week!~~ every night 1 hour.

→ Tech + training mutualy exclusive?

→ Bill £1m O.H per recruit ←how do this?

→ Podcast - who & why on?

→ What tasks delegate or automate?

→ Clarity → why each step?
    → What did I say that inspired?
    → KPI

Milton Keynes UK
Ingram Content Group UK Ltd.
UKHW022240240823
427342UK00008B/148

9 781916 245945